60 0072200 8

KU-181-619

Students an^

DA

27 ^^^^UE F^

Men Out of Work

Men Out of Work

A Study of Unemployment in Three English Towns

M. J. HILL   R. M. HARRISON
A. V. SARGEANT   V. TALBOT

Cambridge
At the University Press 1973

Published by the Syndics of the Cambridge University Press
Bentley House, 200 Euston Road, London NW1 2DB
American Branch: 32 East 57th Street, New York, N.Y. 10022

© Cambridge University Press 1973

ISBN: Hard cover 0 521 20281 7
      Paperback 0 521 09818 1

C C

Set in cold type by E.W.C. Wilkins Ltd,
and printed in Great Britain
at the University Printing House, Cambridge,
(Brooke Crutchley, University Printer).

Contents

Foreword

In 1968, when I was appointed as temporary Social Work Adviser to the Supplementary Benefits Commission, I was asked to examine a number of aspects of the Commission's functions which affected the welfare of individuals. Amongst those which interested me particularly was the problem of so-called 'voluntary unemployment'. The policies of the Supplementary Benefits Commission and the problems which arise from them have been discussed at some length elsewhere.[1] But the discussion was in many aspects speculative, in the absence of research into the nature of the problem and the factors, economic, social and psychological, associated with it. On my return to the University of Oxford in 1970, the Department of Health and Social Security sponsored research under my direction of which the material in this report is the first outcome.

The research falls into two parts; the first, a survey of the factors associated with chronic or frequent unemployment, was completed in 1972 and this book presents the preliminary analysis and discussion of the evidence. The authorship is a joint one and it is the work of the Research Officer, Michael Hill, who was appointed to take charge of the Survey and of our three research assistants, Robert Harrison, Anthony Sargeant and Valerie Talbot. My own role has been purely advisory and, of course, in liaison with the Department of Health and Social Security. The decision to publish a preliminary report was taken during the course of the research; mainly because it became evident that the topic was one of considerable interest to people with different interests and disciplines and one about which there was some urgency. It was also clearly desirable that those who had worked so hard in planning and executing the survey should have the opportunity of contributing to some written conclusions.

However, time has not yet permitted us to analyse and discuss all of the implications of the report: Michael Hill and I will collaborate on a further book which attempts this. In particular, we hope to examine the relations which do or should exist between three aspects of our Social Services which are relevant to the unemployed: namely, the income maintenance services based on contributions (that is, in this country, unemployment and sickness benefit); means-

---

1 Client or Claimant? A Social Worker's View of the Supplementary Benefits Commission. O. Stevenson National Institute Social Services Library, No. 25., Allen & Unwin 1973.

tested benefits which are provided to supplement or replace those benefits (in this country, supplementary benefits); and the personal social work services. As is pointed out in this report, the present structural relations between the Department of Employment and the Supplementary Benefits Commission are somewhat ambiguous. Both have responsibilities which go beyond the payment of benefit. Indeed, so far as the Department of Employment is concerned, there are well advanced plans for a separation of the payment from the 'job finding' function. The Supplementary Benefits Commission also enters the 'job finding' field with and for certain men. The social work services have, by and large, only been involved in these problems as a secondary focus, arising from the primary task (for example, of preventing delinquency or combating poverty). Work, per se, has not been a central issue, except for the handful of social workers employed in Industrial Rehabilitation Units. There are major issues and problems here, upon which this report can only comment superficially and which we shall examine fully later. We shall also provide further information on the attitudes and characteristics of unemployed men, derived from a small sample interviewed in much greater depth and detail than was possible in the main survey.

More light may, in fact, be thrown upon these matters by the second part of the research, now in progress. In this, the work of social workers with unemployed men receiving supplementary benefit is to be compared with that of officials, designated as 'Unemployment Review Officers'. It is not appropriate to describe this here.[1] Suffice it to say that the Research Officer, 'Tom' Thompson and I will collaborate in analysis of these findings which will in some ways complement those of the earlier survey and that the results of the research will be available in 1974.

There is a sense in which the findings of this report may be described as a ground clearing operation: much of it will not surprise those who are knowledgeable through day to day contacts with the unemployed. It does not come as a shock to find that age, lack of skill, and disability are the major factors associated with unemployment in areas of high unemployment. As with much research in the social sciences, the first stage may be to confirm the obvious, with the occasional bonus for the researcher of refuting the apparently obvious. However, it has to be done, for one man's common sense is another man's nonsense. It is particularly important in this field because the topic is a highly emotional one, round which mythologies develop. Politicians of all shades are subject to considerable pressure from public opinion to urge their civil servants

---

1 For an outline of the research plans, see Appendix II to *Client or Claimant.*

to take a harder line with 'the work shy', a pejorative term whose moralistic overtones block further analysis of the problem. This research has been concerned to get behind that phrase and the official equivalent 'the voluntarily unemployed' and to ask the question, 'does such a group exist; if so, what are they like and how do they relate to the labour market?' It is our hope that some of the facts in this report will help those who shape policy, not least by providing concrete evidence to complement experience.

The authors will be specific in their acknowledgements to those who have cooperated in the execution of the research. For my part, I would like to mention in particular Geoffrey Beltram who was, at the time the research was planned, in charge of research development in the Social Security field and whose deep concern about this particular topic was a source of encouragement to me in formulating the research plans.

Olive Stevenson

Acknowledgments

In her forward Olive Stevenson has made clear the role of the Department of Health and Social Security as the sponsors of this research. The relationship between the research team and the DHSS has been a most satisfactory one. Our difficulty, therefore, in acknowledging the help given to us by individual civil servants is that we are indebted to a large number of people, many of whom we have never met and do not know by name. Within the DHSS three groups of people have assisted us with the research. First, there were those from the division (SR5) specifically responsible for liaising with research projects such as ours. Everyone there was most helpful and encouraging. We would however like to single out for special mention Douglas Whiting and Ivor Hughes, who bore much of the responsibility for day to day liaison with us. Second, there were policy makers from a number of divisions who assisted us with their comments on our plans, questionnaire and manuscript. Within that group of people we would like to express our particular thanks to Mary Jones and Peter Harmston. Third, we would like to thank the managers and staff of the DHSS local offices in Swindon, Coventry, Hammersmith and Newcastle, who helped us when we were actually in the field.

From our point of view the Department of Employment had as important a role as the DHSS in assisting us with the many practical aspects of the survey. Their local employment exchange staffs shouldered the overwhelming burden of practical support for the project when we were in the field. We are very grateful for all the help received from the Department of Employment in the three main research areas and the pilot survey area. Despite the fact that they were often excessively busy the local staff always received us in a most friendly and helpful way. We are also grateful to headquarters staff of the Department of Employment, who helped the project to run smoothly and contributed their comments on our efforts.

One other government department should not remain unacknowledged: the Criminal Records Office of the Home Office, who kindly supplied us with data.

In each area the local authorities also provided help on the various occasions when we approached them for information. We would like to thank them for the interest they took in the project.

In running a large scale research project one is inevitably dependent upon the contributions of a large number of people, who are involved in a variety of ways. Most of the secretarial work for the project was done by Mary McMahon and Ann Lincoln-Brown. Their contributions were obviously important ones. We would like to thank the various other people who gave us secretarial help, and the following for the clerical help they gave: Anne Barefoot, John Grainger, Gareth Jones, Harold Lumsden, Barbara Miller, Doreen O'Brien, Dan Parsons and Tom Rivers. We are very grateful for the efforts of our interviewers, who were too numerous to name individually. We would also like to thank Clive Payne, Jean Nicholls and the Research Services Unit of Nuffield College; the Atlas Computer staff; the research services unit of the National Foundation for Educational Research; and Christopher Hill, for their assistance with the computing and statistical work for the project.

We would like to thank those of our colleagues who took a particular interest in the project and in particular Joan Payne, George Smith and 'Tom' Thompson. Olive Stevenson's involvement in the project will, of course, be evident from the foreword, but we would like to express our appreciation of the way in which she has seen her role as involving a combination of a readiness to leave us alone to get on with the day to day work on the project and a willingness to be available for consultation when problems arose.

We have left our most important acknowledgement until last. This is to the men who allowed us to put them 'under the microscope', who freely, and with no hope of personal gain, allowed our interviewers to subject them to a lengthy and sometimes stressful interrogation about their lives and circumstances. The only thing we can offer in return for their crucial co-operation is the hope that this book will make a contribution to a wider understanding of their predicament.

1 Introduction

This book is the first report of a sociological survey, undertaken in Autumn 1971, of unemployed men in three large urban areas, Coventry, Hammersmith and Newcastle upon Tyne. To explain how the approach to the study of employment described in this book developed, it is necessary to review some earlier studies and discussions of the subject. Running through most of the older presentations of the issues is a tendency to separate economic explanations of unemployment from explanations in terms of the characteristics of the individuals involved. Hence there are available either discussions of only one half of the subject, or worse still, explanations which make the assumption that while some unemployment is explicable in purely economic terms, the failure of certain groups to obtain or hold jobs must be the subject of generalisations dealing with social and personal factors.

The nineteenth century Poor Law approach to the problem was largely to disregard economic factors and attribute unemployment solely to the personal failings and faults of individuals, to assume that anyone with the will to work could find work. It was to counteract this view that Beveridge published his *Unemployment: A Problem of Industry* in 1912. In this book he expressed the argument against the traditional view in colourful terms which remind us of the way unemployment was popularly regarded:

> If, therefore, certain degenerate types could be abolished, and if the common level of human nature – in respect of assiduity, sobriety, adaptability, and all other virtues – could be raised, the volume of idleness, whether voluntary or involuntary, would no doubt be diminished. To this extent it is right to urge improvement of human character as a remedy for unemployment. The limitations on this admission have, however, to be carefully noted. First, the number of the entirely unemployable class, though uncertain, is certainly not very great. Second, the most practicable way of improving human character lies often in abolishing industrial and social conditions which induce or pander to the vices of idleness, slovenliness and irresponsibility. Third, no conceivable improvement in the character of the workmen will eliminate the main economic facts in unemployment. (Pp. 137–8)

Another writer of roughly the same period, Charles Booth, in his *Life and Labour of the People of London,* showed a similar sensitivity to the importance

1

of economic factors, but he portrayed perhaps more clearly than Beveridge did, in the piece quoted above, the way in which economic and other factors interact:

> Whilst men in almost every trade work with practically no loss of earnings, and some do so even in the most irregular and uncertain employments, others are habitual half-timers. No point has been more emphatically emphasised by the present enquiry than the unequal efficiency of the members of any industry and the relatively disadvantageous position of the less efficient. To them, competition deals out stern justice, whatever the cause of their inefficiency be.

While we may not warm today to all Booth's explanations of the causes of this inefficiency, there is in this simple statement of his a very clear expression of the way in which the inefficiencies of a capitalist economy have the maximum impact upon the least well equipped individuals. This is a fact that tended to be forgotten as the economists began to dominate the study of unemployment during the massive recession of the 1930s.

Prior to Keynes the orthodox economist's viewpoint corresponded closely with the Victorian doctrine that anyone who is out of work more than temporarily is in some sense at fault. The orthodox analysis of the relationship between wages and unemployment allowed for only two categories of unemployment, 'frictional' and 'voluntary' unemployment. Frictional unemployment was seen as:

> due to a temporary want of balance between the relative quantities of specialised resources as a result of miscalculation or intermittent demand; or to time-lags consequent on unforeseen changes; or the fact that the change-over from one employment to another cannot be effected without a certain delay, so that there will always exist in a non-static society a proportion of resources "between jobs". (J.M. Keynes, quoting Pigou's viewpoint).

Any unemployment that was not frictional must be, it was argued:

> "voluntary" unemployment due to the refusal or inability of a unit of labour, as a result of legislation or social practices or of slow response to change or of more human obstinacy, to accept a reward corresponding to the value of the product attributable to its marginal productivity. (Ibid.)

The importance of Keynes' analysis for the study of unemployment is that he showed how it was possible for what he called 'involuntary' unemployment to occur as a consequence of deficient demand for labour. Those studies of unemployed men which were conducted in the thirties were concerned to

2

make a similar point, though not in terms of academic economics. Both the Pilgrim Trust study and the study of unemployment in Greenwich by E.W. Bakke stressed that the general run of unemployed men showed no signs of being voluntarily unemployed and were in general terms simply typical members of the working class. On the voluntary unemployed, the Pilgrim Trust team argued:

> That there is a certain number of "work-shy" men among the young unemployed is of course not open to doubt, and the question is only what proportion they bear to the whole. In our view, the number is relatively speaking not large, and tends to be exaggerated by confusion with another group, which constitutes a much more troublesome problem, the men who have become diffident owing to continual unemployment, who find it more and more difficult to face repeated failures and who finally give up looking for work. (Pilgrim Trust p. 173)

Bakke took a similar line, putting the problem of malingering in the wider context of the social and economic situation of the time:

> Malingering is mainly a misfit problem. Certain groups fail to be exposed to the influences which develop self-respect in the normal individual, or these influences may be removed through prolonged unemployment. Individuals in these groups, then, are particularly subject to the temptation of malingering.
> Malingering is in the main a negative lack of virtue, not a positive vice. It manifests itself in doing nothing rather than actively plotting to "beat the system"...
> Malingering is the result primarily of the failure of certain behaviour forming influences to function rather than the operation of certain influences productive of an active will to "get all one can". (Bakke, pp. 266–7)

These students of British unemployment were primarily interested in stressing the 'normal' nature of the mass of the unemployed, and were therefore prepared to concede to the Victorian view that there might be a 'pathological' minority within the massive ranks of the unemployed. Inevitably these studies, as more or less the last large-scale sociological studies of unemployment carried out in Britain, did not dispose of the popular view that the voluntarily unemployed, or, more pejoratively, work-shy, would be a social problem again once the problem of mass unemployment was defeated.

There is, naturally, likely to be a small group of men who will freely admit to being voluntarily unemployed. But in addition many members of the general

3

public will allege that there is a much larger class of people who are in fact voluntarily unemployed even though they will not admit to it. The main difficulty in testing this 'theory' is that it is almost impossible to refute, since to do so it is necessary to prove that the men in question cannot behave in any other way than the way they do. Even where it seems possible to 'explain' unemployment by reference to characteristics such as severe disability, it can always be argued that such people could find work if only they tried harder. What is required, therefore, in relation to any hypothesis about voluntary unemployment is a value judgement about the amount of effort individuals should make in order to overcome their disadvantages and handicaps.

In the light of these considerations it is worthy of note that a number of writers have drawn attention to the sources of low motivation on the part of the underprivileged worker. Many years ago Allison Davis drew attention to this issue with reference to the poor in the United States, developing a line of argument that has become a commonplace to students of the Negro poor, which he set out as follows:

> He lives in a different economic and social environment from that in which the skilled and middle-class workers live. Therefore, the behaviour that he learns, the habits that are stimulated and maintained by his cultural group, are different also. The individuals of these different socio-economic statuses and cultures are reacting to different realistic situations and psychological drives. Therefore their values and their social goals are different. Therefore, the behaviour of the underprivileged worker which the boss regards as "unsocialised" or "ignorant", or "lazy", or "unmotivated" is really behaviour learned from the socio-economic and cultural environments of these workers. In a realistic view we must recognise it to be perfectly normal, a sensible response to the conditions of their lives.
>
> If we wish to change their habits ... we must offer the underprivileged workers real rewards. They must be sufficiently powerful to repay him for the hard work and self-denial required to change his old habits, and to compete with the rewards of a physical kind which he clearly gets.
> (A. Davis in W.F. Whyte ed. pp. 103–4)

More recently some economists, particularly in the United States (see Hall, Bosanquet and Doeringer), have seized upon this kind of argument, and have sought to show that some of the peculiarities of the functioning of national labour markets result from the presence of a 'secondary' labour market, which offers insecure and un-rewarding employment to poorly educated and low skilled workers. In this 'market' workers respond to their unsatisfactory economic situations by being unreliable employees, who abandon jobs readily

4

and accept spells of unemployment as a respite from the unwelcome demands of their work situations.

While it is unlikely that the social situation of the British white unemployed worker, living in an area where the overwhelming majority of men are in full-time work, can be entirely equated with that of the underpriviledged in the United States, and particularly with the situation which faces the Negro ghetto dweller, these observations on the relationship between economic situation and motivation serve to remind us of the underlying possibilities of such links. The psychological mechanisms which create and reinforce work habits are bound to be relatively 'fragile' in situations where work is insecure and unrewarding. Therefore, while economic factors do not 'explain' why some individuals have low commitments to work in situations in which other comparable men have high commitments, they suggest that it is not surprising that such attitudes exist.

Another plausible way in which voluntary unemployment is 'explained' rests upon the argument that under certain circumstances it is unprofitable to the individual to work. Interestingly this argument is found in the studies of unemployment done in the thirties, despite the very low levels of benefit and relief available then. The Pilgrim Trust study referred to 'men living at a low level because they have never known anything better'. (Pp. 60—1) 'This particular factor in unemployment', they said, 'can only be attacked as part of the general social problem of poverty—a larger task ... than the attack on unemployment which is sometimes one of its many symptoms'. Similarly Bakke laid considerable emphasis upon the significance of the fact that the unskilled workers secured only a very small margin over their basic needs when in work.

More recently Abel-Smith and Townsend, Atkinson and the Ministry of Social Security report on the Circumstances of Families have drawn attention to the large numbers of families supported by wages below or only just above the income levels provided by Supplementary Benefits scales. When these people fall out of work the Supplementary Benefits Commission is required to ensure that any payments from that source leave them with incomes not exceeding their normal wage levels, but it is open to argument (a) whether this 'wage stopping' is always successful in actually keeping help from all sources during a period of unemployment below potential wages, and (b) whether a relatively slight difference between a wage-stopped allowance and normal earnings is sufficient to offset all the other disincentives to go to work.

In this discussion so far it has been shown that there are considerable difficulties in distinguishing the arguments about unemployment as a consequence of voluntary choice by the unemployed from those about unemployment as an economic phenomenon with an involuntary impact upon individuals. Much

5

the same difficulties reappear with the approach to the explanation of prolonged unemployment as a phenomenon with a 'social' as opposed to an economic cause. This involves the explanation of unemployment in terms of the inadequacies of individuals.

Once a combination of favourable economic circumstances and post-Keynesian management of the economy enabled the unemployment level to be kept at a very low rate, by the standards of the thirties, it tended to be assumed that those who remained unemployed might be considered to come under the two old-fashioned headings of 'frictional' and 'voluntary' unemployment attacked by Keynes.

The concept of frictional unemployment was, at the same time, given a rather more sophisticated meaning. Thus Hauser and Burrows wrote:

> This kind of unemployment accompanies technological progress, the reorganisation of production, and lasting shifts in the pattern of demand. Workers in particular jobs and with particular skills lose their occupations and must seek alternative employment ... . In recent years interest has centred on the relatively high level of frictional unemployment in particular geographical areas and also on the severe impact this unemployment can have on particular sections of the labor force. In its more severe, rather long-term form, frictional unemployment is often referred to as structural unemployment. (M.M. Hauser and P. Burrows, 1969)

Concern with frictional unemployment has particularly focussed upon the rate of labour turnover. Evidence from Department of Employment statistics shows that a high proportion of all the men who register as unemployed remain on that register for only a short period. Fowler studied registrations during the period 1961 to 1965 and showed that of an average of 57,000 new registrants each week '15,000 could expect to leave within a week and 39,000 (or 68 per cent) could expect to leave within four weeks'. Economists who were concerned with raising labour market efficiency therefore concentrated on seeking means to reduce the length of time spent on the register by this large number of men who get back to work fairly quickly (Mackay et al, Reid).

In accordance with this preoccupation there have been a number of studies of redundant workers (Kahn, Wedderburn, 1964 and 1965, Acton Society Trust).

Regional inequalities have been also given considerable attention by economists (Hunter, Brechling), and there has altogether been a different public attitude to unemployment in the least prosperous regions. Although the differences between the regions with high and the regions with low unemployment have been typically only a few percentage points, people are very much

6

more ready to conceptualise unemployment in the North-East, for example, in the same terms as that of the thirties. Hence generalisations about voluntary unemployment or about individual pathology are much less readily applied to such areas. There has only been one study of the social characteristics of unemployed men in such areas, a small one by Sinfield (see Sinfield 1970).

Other unemployment that cannot easily be explained in terms of either slow redeployment or regional pockets of stagnation is often explained by reference to the personal inadequacies of individuals. Professor Paish, resting his analysis upon a Ministry of Labour survey (Ministry of Labour Gazette, 1966, pp. 156–7 and 385–7) in which employment exchange clerks were asked to assess whether their unemployed clientele were 'likely to spend long periods on the register even when the local demand for labour is "high" ', developed a highly simplistic argument on this point. He argued, of the group who were assessed as having poor job prospects, in this way:

> These people, who cannot be regarded as competing effectively for the vacancies available, are put in the Ministry of Labour's survey of October 1964 at over 180,000 or about 0.8% of the employed population, a figure which now may well be higher. These "non-effective" unemployed are distributed very unequally between the regions, with 98,000 or 1.3% of employees, in the North or North-West of England, Scotland and Wales, and only 83,000 or 0.5% in the rest of England. If we deduct the non-effectives ... we reduce the amount of unemployment in the high unemployment area in October, 1967 ... from 254,000 or 3.4% to 156,000 or 2.1% and in the low unemployment area from 307,000 or 1.9% to 224,000 or 1.4%. (Paish, 1968, p. 16)

Paish advised, 'It would clarify the position if the greater part of the non-effectives could be removed from the unemployment figures and transferred to some other register of the welfare state'. (Ibid.) There are several serious flaws in Paish's argument. The figures are based upon assessments made by a large number of junior clerks in the Ministry of Labour, who were asked to make a judgement on a purely hypothetical question; whether their clientele would get work if labour demand were high. It is therefore not surprising that clerks in low labour demand areas differed from those in high demand areas in their judgements, coloured as they must have been by their experience of one specific kind of labour market. Judgements about the 'effectiveness' of individual potential employees cannot really be made in a vacuum. A joint strategy aimed at increasing the attractiveness of so-called non-effective employees to potential employers, increasing the advantages to be gained from going to work for such employees, and increasing the overall demand for labour would

7

inevitably decrease the non-effective numbers. The latter is an approach that has been favoured by those economists who are exponents of the need to adopt an 'active labour market policy' on the lines developed in Sweden (see the description of this approach in Mukherjee, Rehnberg, Olsson and OECD, 1963; and the reflections on the British situation by Thirlwell, and Bosanquet and Standing).

It seems sensible to suggest that at any given level of demand for labour those who cannot get work easily will appear 'less effective' than those who can. This means that in practice it must be difficult to distinguish between 'non-effectives', as described by Paish, and the 'frictionally unemployed', as described by other economists. To pick up the physical analogies implied, it must be recognised that there are degrees of friction up to a sticking point. This is clearly acknowledged in the Report of an Inter-Departmental Working Party on the Unemployment Statistics, where the following objections are raised to suggestions that there is a sizeable class of 'unemployable' people who can be clearly distinguished from the rest of the unemployed:

> It is clear ... that there is some confusion between the meaning of "unemployable" as a description of certain characteristics of a person, and as a description of the "employability" of a person in a particular labour market. It is this confusion which leads to the apparent contradiction that whilst some virtually "unemployable" individuals can be identified, the characteristics of these individuals cannot be used as a basis for the definition of a wider "unemployable" group. In short, the symptom is common to too many ailments to form the basis of a useful diagnosis.
>
> There is a further distinction to be made between the use of the word "unemployable" as a description of a group, and as applied to an individual. The Department of Employment has a duty to do its best to place in work everyone who is registered for employment in as far as this is possible, and it must therefore act on the assumption that everyone is employable. However, it is obvious that some individuals are more employable than others, and that employers are inclined to take a very selective view of the quality of registrants submitted to them.

While it is sensible to expect that employers' selection procedures will tend to sort potential employees in the way assumed by those who talk of 'non-effectives' or 'unemployables', in fact very little is known about the actual impact of such discrimination. Few studies have been made of selection techniques and those there have been have suffered from poor response rates and difficulties in probing beyond official policies. One valuable study that is available (Mackay et al) does, however, suggest that selection procedures are

8

often absent, and that many employers are little concerned to adopt elaborate techniques to ensure that they acquire only the best 'quality' manual employees.

It is therefore dangerous to jump to conclusions about the employability of individuals from information about their characteristics alone. This is a warning that must be given to those who seek to generalise about employment trends from the information presented in this study. In particular it is difficult to relate findings about the quality of the labour 'supply' to currently fashionable theories about technological unemployment without information on the reasons why employers seem to persistently reject some applicants for work.

The purpose of the discussion in this chapter so far has been to analyse some of the difficulties in considering such notions as 'voluntary unemployment' and 'unemployability' or 'ineffectiveness', and to suggest the complex nature of the interaction between economic, social and psychological factors in relation to unemployment. It serves, therefore, both to introduce the present study and to warn against some of the difficulties that are associated with attempts to theorise about the characteristics and attitudes of unemployed men. Since a study of unemployed men of the scale and scope of the present one has not been attempted in Britain since the 1930s, the authors have had to try to address themselves to the mixture of assumptions based on official statistics and folk wisdom that provides almost the only available source of hypotheses in this field, while acknowledging that the complicated relationship between economic and social factors makes theorising difficult. If this study tends to seize upon the simplifications and half-truths that govern public attitudes to unemployment and use these as hypotheses, it is hoped, at least, that it will provide some findings upon which future students of the subject can build more sophisticated hypotheses.

This study was originally conceived as an attempt to throw some light upon long-term unemployment in situations of full employment, by comparing the social characteristics and attitudes of long and short-term unemployed men in situations of comparatively full employment. However, during the planning stage the employment situation worsened, and by the time the field work was due to start in October 1971 unemployment had reached a level almost unprecedented in the post Second World War period. Figure 1 illustrates very clearly the contrast between the 1971 situation and the situation everyone had grown used to in the years before.

This change in the employment situation in itself made it very clear that a sociological study of unemployment needed to take careful note of economic factors. The first group of hypotheses to be tested were concerned with those characteristics of the long-term unemployed which might tend to make them less effective, or less employable, in any situation, while at the same time considering whether differing economic climates had any impact upon the

9

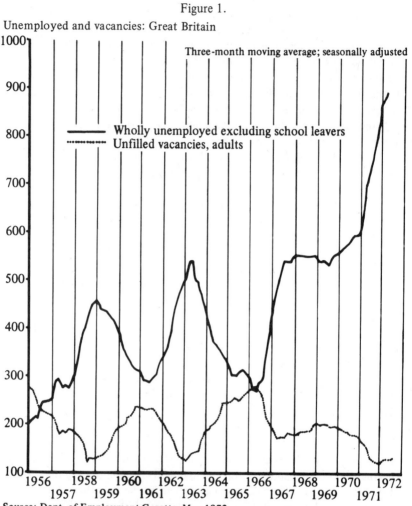

Figure 1.

Unemployed and vacancies: Great Britain

Three-month moving average; seasonally adjusted

—— Wholly unemployed excluding school leavers
········ Unfilled vacancies, adults

Source: Dept. of Employment Gazette, May 1972.

significance of factors of this kind. In drafting this group of hypotheses considerable use was made of the evidence available from published unemployment statistics, and of the evidence brought together from a wide range of countries in Adrian Sinfield's *The Long Term Unemployed.*

Without doubt the strongest evidence available from these sources was on the impact of age upon a man's employment prospects. The figures in Table 1.1 were derived by relating Department of Employment statistics on numbers unemployed in July 1971 to numbers in the work force.

The figures here for the youngest group are perhaps a little misleading, as

10

Table 1.1   Unemployment Rates for Specific Age Groups July 1971

Age Groups	Unemployment Rates	Long-term Unemployment Rates (over 26 weeks)
Up to 29	5.4	0.7
30–9	3.7	1.0
40–9	3.2	1.1
50–9	3.5	1.6
60+	7.0	4.2
All	4.7	1.6

Source: Department of Employment Gazette

the numbers in the work force in that group are affected by numbers of students, and accordingly the unemployed proportion is probably slightly exaggerated. However, the relation between increasing age and increasing long-term unemployment is quite unambiguous. It was hypothesized, therefore, that there would be a strong relation between age and unemployment length, and that age would be a factor that would have to be taken into account and 'held constant' when many other variables were considered.

It was similarly hypothesized that health would be related to unemployment length. Suggestions for this came as much from 'common sense' deductions as from available data. Sinfield's book and the studies of redundant workers provided some advance evidence on this topic. It was decided to try to study this factor by reference to official records of claims for sickness benefits, as well as by seeking evidence directly from men on their disabilities and illnesses. It was also hypothesized that mental health would have an impact upon unemployment length, and accordingly it was decided to try to achieve the independent assessment of this factor.

Next, a group of hypotheses were developed on the relation between occupational skill and unemployment length. It is difficult to extract a great deal of information on this relation from the published unemployment statistics. However, as Table 1.2 suggests, there is reason to suspect that labourers are a markedly disadvantaged group in the employment market.

Bosanquet and Standing, in their analysis of the extent of unemployment amongst various occupational groups, provide supporting evidence on this issue. Their evidence is based upon 1966 census data projected forward to 1970, on the assumption that with a changed unemployment rate the various occupational groups nevertheless remain in the same proportions. Their estimates are given in Table 1.3.

Table 1.2.   Unemployed Labourers October 1971

	Labourers as a percentage all wholly unemployed men	Ratio of unemployed labourers to unfilled vacancies for labourers
Great Britain	53.7	49 to 1
South-East Region	36.4	11 to 1
West Midlands	48.6	101 to 1
Northern Region	64.6	214 to 1

Source: Department of Employment Gazette

Table 1.3.   Estimated Unemployment Rates for Men in Various Occupational Groups—1970

	%
General rate	3.6
Employers and managers	1.9
Professionals	1.1
Intermediate non-manual	2.0
Junior non-manual	3.0
Personal service workers	6.7
Foremen and supervisors	1.7
Skilled manual	2.5
Unskilled	9.3
Farmers	1.3
Agricultural workers	3.4

Source: Bosanquet and Standing

It is possible to achieve an even more up to date estimate using the same procedure; this gives a rate of 13.4% for unskilled men when the male unemployment rate reached 5.2% in October 1971. Bosanquet and Standing applied the same procedure to estimate unemployment rates for unskilled men in the depressed regions. By this method they suggested that the 1970 rate for unskilled men in the Northern region was 15.2%; this suggests a rate of 21.6% by October 1971.

For the present study, therefore, it was hypothesized that unemployment length would be related to occupation and skill. It was decided, too, that it would be advantageous to study these factors from as wide a range of perspectives as possible, taking note of job histories and men's perceptions of their own occupations, as well as formal qualifications and experience and the Department of Employment's own assessments of the skills of the unemployed men.

It was also hypothesized that men's unemployment lengths might be affected by discrimination against them on account of their national or racial origins. Similar considerations applied to discrimination against ex-criminals, though here it was recognized that evidence on employment difficulties might be difficult to interpret, because of the relevance of motivational factors as well as direct discrimination. It is appropriate to point out here that while this complication is more apparent as far as men with criminal records are concerned, it is relevant to some degree to all the apparently 'hard' data analyzed. The source of information on criminal records was the Home Office's Criminal Records Office. Criminal records were made available to the researchers on the condition that strict precautions were taken to ensure that the records were used only for statistical analysis in which specific individuals were unidentifiable.

The second group of hypotheses to be tested related very much more to motivational factors, and therefore to the arguments about voluntary unemployment outlined at the beginning of this chapter. These factors will be considered under three headings: (a) factors related to the theory about low incentives set out earlier, (b) factors which can broadly be seen as requiring the direct investigation of attitudes, and (c) factors related to poverty and deprivation which may possible be seen as causally related to low motivation and morale.

The general hypothesis about incentive situations was expressed earlier as 'that under certain circumstances it is unprofitable to the individual to work'. The testing of this required the examination of the relation between income when out of work and income normally received or expected in work. This hypothesis is often linked in popular judgements with the high social security income received by men with large families, hence examination of family sizes and commitments was also required.

There are a number of different approaches possible to the study of attitudes in this context. It was decided to ask direct questions about commitment to seeking work and the extent of selectivity. At the same time the likelihood that individuals would respond to such questions in the way they supposed the researchers expected, or at least in the way they supposed the official sponsors of the research required, was expected to reduce the value of such a direct approach. Therefore a variety of indirect approaches were also developed, involving questions about job-seeking methods, reasons for losing jobs, willingness to move home or to work away from home, and willingness to accept

13

training. It was also hypothesized that men who had already moved away from the town of their birth would be more highly motivated, or at least likely to be more flexible about where they worked or what they did.

Finally, it was hypothesized that the long-term unemployed may be regarded as a sub-group of a wider class of poor people who experience a variety of deprivations, including continuing low income (whether in or out of work) and inadequate housing. There was an interest in studying these characteristics of the unemployed to provide straightforward information on their circumstances, but it was also felt that it was necessary to throw light on problems of low motivation. In the same way the extent to which the unemployed men were aware of the services and benefits available to them, and were prepared to make use of them, was seen as worthy of investigation.

To complete this introductory chapter it is necessary to provide some information on the factors that influenced the approach adopted to the definition and measurement of long-term unemployment, the selection of the research areas, and the selection of the samples.

There are two straightforward approaches to selecting a sample of unemployed men in order to compare unemployment lengths. One of these is the approach adopted by Fowler, outlined earlier in this chapter, of following up cohorts of newly registered unemployed people. This approach revealed that comparatively few of the people who register for work remain out of work for long periods, so that any sample selected by this method would contain large numbers of short-term and few long-term unemployed. The second approach involves taking a sample of all the people registered as unemployed on a certain date. This is an approach comparable to that adopted by the Department of Employment when it compiles its standard monthly statistics of unemployment. The results achievable by this approach can be predicted, therefore, from the published statistics. In October 1971 32.9% of all the men on the unemployment register had been out of work over 26 weeks, and 18.4% had been out of work over a year. These figures were fairly typical of the proportion in these 'long-term' categories over the past 3 or 4 years, both figures having varied no more than about 4% either way.

In selecting the sample for this research it was decided that the sampling frame should be the whole unemployment register, since this would ensure the inclusion within the sample of a reasonable number of long-term unemployed. However, it was felt necessary to take into account the fact that at any time a certain number of the 'short-term' unemployed are in fact destined to remain out of work for a long time. Accordingly it was decided that in order to compute the 'unemployment length' of the men in the sample, their unemployment during the six months following their selection should be taken into account as well as their unemployment before selection.

14

This procedure and its consequences are described more fully at the beginning of Chapter 3; it has been introduced here to explain why it is inevitable that this study appears to over-emphasize the amount of long-term unemployment as compared with the official statistics, and particularly as compared with studies of unemployment which adopt Fowler's approach to sample selection. This does not mean that it is 'biased', but merely that in a situation in which there are a number of different and equally valid ways of portraying unemployment lengths, an approach has been adopted which facilitates the most thorough scrutiny of the long-term unemployed, while still including many short-term unemployed for purposes of comparison. A cross section sample designed in this way enables a study of long-term unemployment without the adoption of any arbitrary definition of that phenomenon.

In selecting the research areas considerations of cost, together with a need to ensure that economic background factors were taken into account, precluded any attempt to achieve a national sample. It was decided instead to confine attention to three large urban areas. One consequence of this was that in each area studied the employment structure was diverse and the range of job opportunities very wide. It would have been interesting to have included a smaller area where a far narrower range of jobs was available (see Mackay et al), but in such an area the long-term unemployed would have been few in number unless unemployment were very high.

The areas selected for the research project were, as has been stated, the County Boroughs of Newcastle upon Tyne and Coventry and the London Borough of Hammersmith. At the time the research was planned both Coventry and Hammersmith had unemployment rates below the national average. Newcastle was included as a contrasting area with above average unemployment. However, during the months immediately prior to going into the field unemployment rose markedly in Coventry, making it a town with unemployment close to the national average. Coventry has been portrayed as a town with an unemployment rate dramatically above average (see for example the Sunday Times article by Nicholas Faith on 26 September 1971). This is a little misleading because its very high figures arose from the inclusion of the large number of 'temporarily stopped' men in its statistics. However it is interesting in being a town where employment prospects have been very good in recent years, but which has felt the impact of the current recession markedly. More or less by accident, therefore, a situation was provided in which three areas were compared, one with continuing low unemployment, one with persistent high unemployment, and one with current high unemployment but a history of low unemployment.

The samples interviewed were proportions (one-tenth in Newcastle and Coventry, one-fifth in Hammersmith) of all the men wholly unemployed living

15

in the three boroughs and registered at employment exchanges on 1 October 1971. It is recognized that the choice of the unemployment registers as sampling frames provides an incomplete sample of the unemployed as a whole. It tends to exclude some of the most economically secure men, some newly unemployed men, some men between 60 and 65 who are already drawing pensions from previous employers but who still hope to get work, and some men whose ways of life or attitudes lead to them avoiding appearing in official 'registers' wherever possible (see the Report of an Inter-Departmental Working Party on the Unemployment Statistics for further discussion of these omissions). However, to include these men a population survey would have had to be undertaken; this would have been a very expensive and difficult way to minimize this particular bias. In the same way it might have been valuable to have surveyed women as well as men, but had this been done a choice would have had to be made between taking what would undoubtedly have been a very unrepresentative sample of unemployed women from those who register, or once again adopting the unwieldy population sample approach. Finally on this subject, it should be pointed out that the sample was of men over 18. A study of the 15–18 age group would have had to be concerned with somewhat different issues, and once again the problem of achieving a truly representative sample would have cropped up; for this is an age group some of whom choose to remain in full-time education solely because of the lack of jobs. A special study of youth unemployment is badly needed. It was with some regret that it was learnt that the Department of Employment was unable to support a study of this subject, planned by Manchester University, which would have been complementary to this study.

In each area the response rate was approximately 75%. It is difficult to do more than speculate on the biases resulting from this incomplete response, which is nevertheless quite high for a survey of this kind. A comparison of the characteristics of the samples with information collected by the Department of Employment, in the course of undertaking their monthly counts in the areas, suggests that it is not seriously unrepresentative. After the pilot survey, conducted in Swindon, the Department of Employment undertook a brief analysis of the non-respondents. This suggested that men who had gone back to work quickly were under-represented in the sample, but that otherwise there were no obvious biases arising from non-response. It would have been valuable to have analysed non-respondents in the main survey, but the rules about confidentiality meant that this exercise would have had to be carried out by the local officers of the Department of Employment, who had already done a great deal to assist with the research at a time when their normal work load was excessively high.

One group which was suspected of having been under-represented was a relatively small group of men, with very unstable ways of life, who were, at the time the sample was drawn, living in short-stay hostels and lodging houses. Many of these men had moved on to unknown addresses before the interviewers could contact them.

In this chapter a general account has been provided of the various theoretical and methodological considerations that affected the conducting of the survey reported in this book. The next chapter presents information on the three research areas, and ends with a brief description of the men who were interviewed. Chapters 3, 4 and 5 then examine the evidence collected in more detail. The findings are not set out exactly as foreshadowed by the account of the hypotheses above. This is because many of the pieces of evidence analysed have to be related to more than one hypothesis. Chapter 3 is primarily concerned with the main characteristics of the men and the relation of these to unemployment length. Chapter 4 deals largely with the men's circumstances, while Chapter 5 is largely concerned with their attitudes. In Chapter 6 a multi-variate analysis technique is used to throw more light on the relative importance of the main factors and on their inter-relation. Finally Chapter 7 brings together the main conclusions and discusses current policies towards the unemployed with reference to the problems of the longer-term groups.

2 The research areas[1]

Coventry

Coventry is located in a very advantageous commercial position close to the centre of the major population and industrial concentrations in England and Wales. After Birmingham it is the largest city in the Midlands, and up to 1966 it had been the most rapidly expanding city in terms of population. This expansion has mainly been due to the prosperity of Coventry, since 50% of the growth of population is due to immigrants. This has meant that Coventry has a generally younger population, with the inevitable repercussions for the fertility rate leading to further population increase.

The 1966 Census indicated that just over 11% of the population came from outside the United Kingdom. The largest group of immigrants from one country were those from the Irish Republic, who accounted for 5.3% of the total population. The combined groups from the Commonwealth countries with black populations were 3.3% of the total. The main groups of internal immigrants came from Scotland and Wales and were almost equally represented in numbers. These two groups constituted about 3% of the population. The present total population of Coventry is 335,000.

The social structure of Coventry is significantly different from the greater part of the United Kingdom. In 1966 13.6% of the economically active or retired males in Coventry were in the Registrar General's categories I and II. For England and Wales the figure was 20% for these two groups. Social class III in Coventry accounted for no less than 55% of the population, as opposed to 48% for England and Wales. Of the remaining population 22.4% were semi-skilled and 7% unskilled, compared with 19.1% and 8.5% respectively for England and Wales.

Coventry has become widely recognised as a boom city. There is no doubt that compared with other parts of the United Kingdom Coventry is very prosperous. Car ownership is above the national average, although this is probably

---

1 The discussion of the three areas is based primarily upon 1966 census data, together with information collected by the Department of Employment. In addition use has been made of material, both published and unpublished, collected by the planning authorities in each area. We are grateful to the three local authorities and to the Department of Employment for the help they gave in this respect.

not a very good indicator in a city which has 30% of its total work force employed in the car industry. Car workers can buy from their employers at a reduced rate. However, in addition to car ownership, wage rates and home ownership are above the national average. In 1966 59% of the city's housing was owner-occupied, compared with 50% for the U.K. as a whole. Male manual workers in the West Midlands had average weekly earnings of £38 per week in April 1971. Furthermore the West Midlands, of which Coventry is typical, has the highest proportion of double incomes in the country. The average earnings of all men in the West Midlands in April 1971 were £33.8, the figure being brought down by the lower earnings of non-manual workers.

Methods of determining wage rates were a source of considerable controversy during the period of the survey. The main source of disagreement centred on the 'Coventry Tool Room Agreement', which, according to some, created inflationary wage rates. However, if the wage rates are high it cannot be claimed to be solely the result of one type of agreement as opposed to another, because the structure and nature of Coventry's industry makes it very likely that there will be a high earning potential.

Firstly, in 1966 two-thirds of all those employed in manufacturing were employed in ten firms, which each possessed more than £20 million in assets. In addition to this factor the items produced by Coventry's industry are generally the products of highly skilled and precision engineering, resulting in a high value per unit production. These two factors make it very likely that Coventry workers will receive higher remuneration than workers elsewhere.

In addition to the advantages already mentioned, the residents of Coventry also enjoy generally much better housing standards than in many other parts of the country. In 1966 more than 38% of the housing stock in the United Kingdom was over 50 years old, whereas only just over half this percentage were that old in Coventry. Nonetheless Coventry is not without its housing problems, since 25% of all households were lacking one or more basic amenities; that is hot water, a fixed bath and an internal w.c. The largest proportion of these, as would be expected, were living in the pre-1914 dwellings which represent about 25% of the total stock. Over a quarter of Coventry's houses were rented from the Local Authority, 15% were privately rented and 59% were owner-occupied.

The location of housing and industry, assuming workers like to live close to their place of work, is quite convenient. A study undertaken in 1966 indicated that 70% of the population lived within three miles of their place of employment. The largest concentration of industry is also in the same area as the oldest housing. The firms in this area also tend to be smaller ones who provide work for the unskilled lower paid workers. Conversely the industry, i.e. the motor industry, employing the more affluent car owning workers is located in the outer suburbs of the city. The people that have to travel outside

19

the city to work are a small proportion of the total work force in the region, 6% in 1966. In fact nearly three times as many people come into the city to work as travel out.

Employment in Coventry has been declining, as it has for the country as a whole, since 1966. Although there had been some improvement in Coventry during 1969–70, this disappeared at the beginning of 1971. This is clearly illustrated in the graph below.

Figure 2.1.   Graph showing wholly unemployed in Coventry excluding school leavers and temporarily stopped October 1968 to January 1972

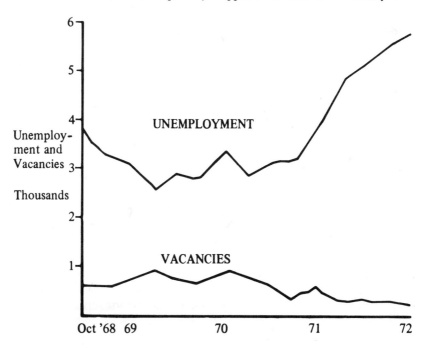

Source of data: Department of Employment

The change in the unemployment figures in 1971 was extremely traumatic for the residents of Coventry, for not only did the absolute position change, but the relative position also altered. The city had up to this point a virtually unbroken 40 year record of unemployment below the national average.

The first and foremost employment problem of Coventry is that it rests on a very narrow industrial base. Employment is very heavily dependent on

20

manufacturing industry. In 1966 63% of the total work force was employed in manufacturing and 53% of the total was employed in four types of industry. These industries were motor vehicle manufacturing (28% of all jobs in Coventry), mechanical engineering (11%), electrical engineering (9%) and aircraft manufacturing (6%). Since 1966 the aircraft industry has declined while the motor vehicle industry has increased in importance as an employer. The dependence on manufacturing is even greater if only male employment is considered. In 1969 75% of all insured males were employed in manufacturing. Apart from the main employment mentioned, other significant employers in the manufacturing sector are component, machine tool and textile manufacturers. Not only is there a situation of nearly all the eggs being in a few baskets, there is a further disadvantage which stems from the fact that these industries are linked, so that if one suffers all may suffer. This dependence on manufacturing makes the employment situation in Coventry very sensitive to changes in national and international economies.

However, if Coventry does have a great dependence on manufacturing, it can at least be said that those industries it does have are generally within the growth sector of the economy. Within the 'Coventry and Solihull' sub-region of Warwickshire, 42% of all employment is in nationally growing industries. If one adds to these industries which are nationally stable, but growing at a faster rate than average within the sub-region, then the figure becomes 54%. Of the remaining 46% which are in line with national growth rates only 19% are in nationally declining industries.

The sub-region does not have its full share of all growth industries because of the over-representation of motor vehicles. In Coventry this is thirteen times greater than it is for the United Kingdom as a whole. However, the proportion of the total industry within the growth sector is greater than for the country as a whole, while it is under-represented in its share of declining industry. Within the declining sector coal mining and the aircraft industry have suffered more than a proportional share of contraction. The aircraft industry is the more important of the two as far as Coventry is concerned. In terms of total employment the declining sector accounts for 13%, of which 5% is aircraft and coal mining.

The comparative advantages of growth enjoyed by the Coventry sub-region are well illustrated by Table 2.1, which shows that between 1961 and 1966 total employment within the area increased by 8.36%, compared with 3.56% in the U.K. as a whole.

The period 1961 to 1966 can be clearly seen as the crest of the boom experienced by Coventry. Since 1966 there has been a steady decline.

There does not appear to be any one single factor which can be put forward to explain Coventry's change in relative position with regard to employment

21

Table 2.1.   Employment data for Great Britain and the sub-region
              1961–6

| | Sub-region % Change | | G.B. % Change | |
	Per Annum	Total	Per Annum	Total
Mining	−4.8	−21.69	−4.9	−22.34
Manufacturing	0.78	3.28	0.1	0.51
Service	3.4	18.31	1.3	6.86
All industries	1.6	8.36	0.7	3.56

in 1971. The total number of redundancies suffered was not as great as in other single years in the past. Neither was there any one single closure or massive redundancy which would account for the sudden jump in unemployment figures.

It would seem that Coventry is not just a city which was badly hit by the 1971–2 depression, but that it has a very much reduced ability to cope with unemployment than in the past. A key factor is no doubt the massive reduction of the aircraft industry in the early sixties. This particular industry had been shedding labour in quite considerable amounts, over the whole country, but in Coventry the contraction was nearly three times as much as elsewhere. During the period 1961–66 employment in the aircraft industry declined by 18.04%, while in Coventry the decline was 50.84%. The total number of jobs lost in this industry alone was greater than the total number of unemployed at the time of the survey.

Another industry that has suffered in Coventry is the machine tool industry, which has been undergoing a process of rationalisation. This industry is responsible for approximately 10% of employment in Coventry and it is fortunate that it is not responsible for more, since the continued lack of invest-ment over the last few years has hit this industry quite badly, resulting in the displacement of many highly skilled men, as was the case with the aircraft industry.

Analysis of unemployment by occupation would seem to uphold the argument that it is the contraction of the types of jobs provided by these industries which has affected Coventry's relative employment position, since it is the relative position of skilled engineering workers that appears to have changed most during the period 1968–71. If 1968 is treated as the base line, 100, then total unemployment rose to 158, while unemployment for skilled workers reached 205 by the end of 1971.

However, while the skilled engineering workers have suffered the greatest

22

change in their relative position, it is very important to emphasise that they are still by no means the group that suffers the greatest incidence of unemployment. The unskilled workers, as everywhere, experience the greatest incidence of unemployment whether times are good or bad. Furthermore, in Coventry the ratio of unemployed to vacancies was considerably worse for unskilled workers than for skilled workers, as Table 2.2 makes clear.

Table 2.2.   Unemployed men and vacancy ratios December 1971

Skilled Construction Workers	8 : 1
Skilled Engineering Workers	26 : 1
Clerical Workers	12 : 1
Labourers	150 : 1

(Figures derived from Department of Employment data)

Some differentiation should be made between labourers within different industries; for some groups in building the situation was only as bad as 5 or 12 : 1, but for most, the situation was far worse, with ratios of 528 : 1 for labourers in engineering and allied trades, and 453 : 1 for light general labourers.

A factor relevant to Coventry's unemployment position in 1971 may have been the Department of Trade and Industry's powers to grant or refuse Industrial Development Certificates (I.D.C.). Briefly, this system controls the creation of new firms or the expansion of old ones where the occupation of more than 5,000 square feet (3,000 before 1970) of additional factory space is involved. The Department of Trade and Industry has stated that applications for I.D.Cs from the West Midlands 'will for the most part be examined critically', (Trade and Industry July 1971). Many local industrialists blamed the change in Coventry's relative employment position on Government regional policies, and in particular on the I.D.C. system. Not unnaturally, while most of them did not dispute the goals of regional policy, they regretted what they believed to be its adverse effect on Coventry. This view, although strongly and widely held, was not supported by any concrete evidence. From 1966 to 1971 there were only a total of six refusals against 277 acceptances. The estimate of jobs created by successful applications was 2,420.

Those who claimed that I.D.Cs have had an adverse effect in Coventry argued, however, that these figures did not represent the true picture. They did not record those who did not get as far as making an application because they expected to meet certain failure. This argument is plausible but not provable.

It should also be considered that not only negative forces should be taken into account, since there were other incentives to go elsewhere, such as lower wage and rent costs plus government grants. It may well be the case that the I.D.C. policy is more a thorn in the side of existing employers who wish to expand their production in the same area, since it is less profitable to have production units split up. This is particularly so for the motor car industry and other industries employing continuous production techniques. It is claimed that Chrysler feel particularly affected, since car bodies are produced in Lynwood, Scotland and transported to Coventry at heavy expense.

It has been estimated that in the 25 years up to 1965 the region generated 68,000 jobs within the manufacturing industries that were exported or steered from it to the Development Areas. (Report on the West Midlands Regional Study: 1971). No doubt a significant proportion of these jobs came from Coventry. Certainly up to 1965 the region could well afford to contribute to employment elsewhere. Since then the situation has changed. The West Midlands study (ibid) estimated that the region had lost 40,000 jobs during the period 1967—70. This had been due not only to a reduction in the growth of the manufacturing industries, but also to a lack of growth in the service sector, together with a decline in mining and agriculture.

To summarise: the situation in Coventry was not that employment was by 1971 relatively bad as compared with other parts of the country, but that really in the past it had been relatively so good. Unemployment slightly above the national average in 1971 was exactly what one might expect to find in a city with Coventry's type of industrial structure. Manufacturing industry, with its direct dependence on consumer demand, is very sensitive to changes in the economic climate. Therefore, with the biggest economic recession since the war, it is not surprising that Coventry felt the pinch just a little more than average. In the past the ability to weather economic depressions had probably been much better there on account of the heavy demand for labour, but with the big reduction in the aircraft industry together with the rationalisation in the machine tool industry, Coventry no longer possessed the ability to shield itself from economic fluctuations as it did in the fifties and early sixties.

Nonetheless, there were few grounds for excessive pessimism in Coventry. It is quite likely that in the future it will follow the fortunes of the country as a whole, while possibly faring a little worse than average until the imbalance in the industrial structure is significantly changed. However, generally the prospects are very bright. That industry which Coventry does have is for the greater part thriving, while at the same time it has a young and highly skilled population.

24

Hammersmith

Hammersmith is the most western of the Inner London boroughs north of the river and is intermediate in location between the principal employment areas of central London and the outer London boroughs of Ealing and Hounslow. With a population in 1966 of 203,240 persons and an area covering no more than 3,995 acres, it is one of the most densely populated boroughs in London. Local Authority boundaries in London are, however, mainly an administrative convenience, journey to work patterns being intricate and commuting across the conurbation the normal order of the day. Hammersmith is therefore as much a dormitory area for those working elsewhere in London (57% of the resident occupied population cross the borough boundaries to work) as an employment area for those living both inside and outside the borough.

London's high level of employment has traditionally attracted immigrants both from this country and overseas, and it is towards the relief of resulting social pressures and the correction of the imbalance between employment in London and the rest of the country that decentralisation policies have been aimed. Until recently, employment policy for London has been based upon the assumption that its economy would continue to grow at a rate which would provide sufficient jobs for its own labour force together with a surplus for other areas. However, the success of measures taken to divert both industry and population from London — and most notably the marked and continued fall in the population — has led to a re-evaluation of policy, which, it is now suggested, should prevent any further fall in the labour supply and encourage growth selectively in the industries which perform best in the capital.

The analysis of employment changes within London is complicated by both the flows of labour between sectors and the difficulty of deriving data for meaningful employment areas. For the most part, therefore, it is necessary to place Hammersmith against the background of the employment situation in London as a whole, although some tentative observations at a local level can be made with the help of research carried out for the Greater London Plan.

Since 1951 London's growth rate has been steadily declining, the Outer Metropolitan Area and the South East Region as a whole benefiting from the industries which have moved out of London. Over the period 1961–6 the decrease in employment accelerated still further, London's economy growing by an annual rate of only 0.2% compared with 1.4% in England and Wales and 3.3% for the rest of the region. The industries which have experienced the greatest decline are those in the manufacturing group, predominantly engineering, which contributed 32.5% to the total fall in employment in those industries; service industries over the same period expanded. The contraction in manufacturing has resulted in an overall decrease in male employment of −0.4% annually, while female employment, boosted by expansion in services, has risen. (see Table 2.3)

As is shown in Table 2.4, male unemployment in manufacturing increased by 33.1% during the years 1961−6, compared with 3.0% for Great Britain as a whole. Although male unemployment rose slightly in all occupational groups (and notified vacancies decreased) those hardest hit in 1966 remained unskilled operatives, as five years earlier; supply also exceeded demand for male office clerks. The greatest demand for male labour was for skilled transport workers, skilled operatives and administrative office workers.

Table 2.3. Average annual changes in employment in Greater London 1961−6

Industry	Males		Females		Total	
	No.	% Annual Change	No.	% Annual Change	No.	% Annual Change
Primary	−	−	−	−	−	−
Manufacturing	−95,000	−2.0	−30,000	−1.2	−125,000	−1.7
Construction	+24,000	+1.9	+6,000	+6.8	+30,000	+2.2
Services	+18,000	+0.2	+124,000	+2.3	+142,000	+1.1
Total	−53,000	−0.4	+100,000	+1.3	+47,000	+0.2

Table 2.4. Changes in male and female unemployment by industry groups: Greater London and Great Britain September 1961−6

Industry	Greater London			Great Britain		
	Males %	Females %	Total %	Males %	Females %	Total %
Primary	+16.7	−57.1	+6.7	+27.9	−14.8	+23.9
Manufacturing	+33.1	−34.1	+13.0	+3.0	−28.0	−6.0
Construction	+31.6	+21.2	+31.5	+30.4	+33.6	+30.4
Services	+6.3	−38.3	−7.6	+17.2	−7.3	+9.0
Total	+16.0	−37.1	+1.2	+15.4	−14.3	+7.3

An analysis of supply and demand by sector made by the G.L.C. suggests that both the overall demand for labour and the demand for labour of certain occupational types varies within London. In particular, the inner sector's share of the total employment of the conurbation has continued to fall while employment has expanded in parts of outer London. In April 1966, the inner sector was the only one in London where recorded vacancies were less than the unemployed, the area having 49.0% of London's unemployment and 21.9% of its vacancies. It is here that it is suggested that opportunities are most limited for the semi-skilled and unskilled, as the vacancies in the central area are not suitable and there is little evidence to suggest, on the basis of present journey to work patterns, that these people will commute to alternative work-places. (*Greater London Development Plan,* 1969, Para. 3.166). In the Hammersmith area at the time of the survey, the unskilled (labourers) constituted 34.2% of the male unemployment register, clerical workers 9.8% and those seeking administrative and professional positions 10.6%. Hammersmith falls into part of the inner sector (the north west), where in 1970 the ratio of unfilled vacancies to unemployment was low in comparison with the London average. However, it is possible that, while Hammersmith's labour force has been affected by the decline in employment opportunities in the inner sector, this has to some extent been offset by accessibility to the outer west of London where demand for labour, especially for operatives, is above average.

Hammersmith is strategically sited both in relation to the national road network and to the primary road network of greater London. Major routes into London from the west pass through the borough and the recently built Western Avenue extension provides links with the M1 and the north. If the proposals put forward in the Development Plan are carried out, the western section of London's inner ringway will be built within its boundaries. Ease of communications and proximity to Heathrow Airport would seem therefore to offer favourable locations for industry and commerce. Several national concerns, such as the J. Lyons Group, G. Wimpey and Company, and the British Oxygen Company, have their headquarters in the borough and the BBC is a large employer. Developments planned for the future include the building of a new airline terminal with hotel facilities and the terminal for the Channel Tunnel.

The principal employing industries in Hammersmith are those which dominate London as a whole, although there are differences in the relative importance of each. Service industries, which have been the growing point in the economies of London and the South East generally, are an even greater source of employment in Hammersmith (they employ 20.4% of the working population compared with 13.9% in Greater London), but the proportions working in distributive trades and professional and scientific services (next in order of importance)

27

are close to the average. There is more food manufacture and construction in Hammersmith while engineering/electrical goods and transport and communication are less prominent.

As indicated earlier, however, the borough as an area of employment is of only partial concern, over half of the resident work-force being employed elsewhere in London. For the most part, Hammersmith residents travel to the boroughs immediately to the east and west to work, more than half to Westminster and Kensington and smaller proportions (13% and 6%) to Ealing and Hounslow; the areas to the north and south are rather less important. Women constitute a greater proportion of the work force than in London generally, and are more likely than men to live and work in the borough, but the activity rates are above average for males and females.

The socio-economic structure of Hammersmith is in most respects close to the London average, which in turn differs from England and Wales in the high proportion of non-manual workers, both of intermediate and professional/ managerial status. In Hammersmith, the largest groups proportionately are skilled manual (35.9%) and junior non-manual workers (23.4%), similar to London as a whole, but there are less in the professional/managerial groups and more manual workers when the unskilled and semi-skilled are included. Hammersmith is therefore somewhat intermediate in socio-economic characteristics between the professional character of Central London and the more homogeneous working class boroughs such as Southwark and Tower Hamlets. Clerical work and services are the dominant occupations but the services categories are over-represented; there are also rather more labourers and slightly less in professional and technical occupations.

In general, the tendency is for the resident population to work in services, sales, and manual employment, while those commuting into Hammersmith to work are more likely to be in administrative and professional positions. There are some differences too in the occupational structure of the two work streams which make up the total resident labour force, although this may be partly accounted for by the greater number of women living and working in the borough: more of those employed in Hammersmith work in services and sales occupations and to a lesser extent, construction, but those travelling outside of the borough to work are more likely to be employed in clerical occupations and engineering and allied trades. The socio-economic groupings show an even clearer divide with more commuters in the junior non-manual and supervisory/ skilled manual groups and more of those working in Hammersmith in semi-skilled and unskilled occupations and 'own account' workers.

There is no information on earnings in Hammersmith, but the number of earners to the household is standard for London — which is slightly above the level for the rest of the country. Earnings in London are, however, higher than

28

in Great Britain as a whole and more than in the South East region; in April 1971 full time male adults earned an average of £38.00, £31.06 for manual workers and £44.5 for those in non-manual occupations. Earnings were higher in Central London than in the rest of the conurbation.

Environmentally, Hammersmith is dominated by its communications, the meeting of east-west and north-south routes combining to produce some of the heaviest traffic flows in London. Prior to 1965, the north and the south of the borough were administered separately under the old scheme of London government and the two areas still retain a certain division of function; Fulham with its long river frontage is more diverse industrially and provides wharfage and sites for manufacture, while Hammersmith tends to be the commercial and administrative centre of the borough. Many of Hammersmith's social problems are those typically associated with inner London: population turn-over is high, and much of the private housing sector, which accommodates 65% of households in the borough, is seriously deficient in basic amenities. Overcrowding is above the average for London. In spite of the high rates of in-migration, however, Hammersmith's population is continuing to fall. Between 1961 and 1966, the population declined by 8.5%, compared with 2% for London as a whole, and by 1970 it was estimated to have fallen still further to 187,980.

Because of heavy migration flows, the demographic and housing characteristics of greater London are in some ways significantly different from those in the country as a whole, reflecting the greater attraction of London for the young and single and the relative disadvantages for families with children:

> A disproportionately large number of young adults 15–24, who have the highest expectance of marriage, come into London and a disproportionately large number in the age-ranges 25–44 move out (Greater London Development Plan 1969, Para. 2.29).

In Hammersmith, the proportion of adults in their twenties is above the London average (17.5% compared with 14.1%) and that of the 39–44 age-group less. More of the population are single and there are more households consisting of non-related members (34.3% as against 24.1%). Hammersmith also has a higher immigrant population; the main immigrant groups are the Southern Irish (7.2%), those born in Commonwealth countries (8.0%) and other foreigners (4.7%).

Household size in London is smaller than the national average and in Hammersmith, where the proportion of young unattached adults is above that for London as a whole, even less. The resulting high demand for small units of accommodation is made effective by multiple occupation of large dwellings, of which London has an above average proportion. In Hammersmith, multiple

29

occupation is one of the most marked features of the local housing situation, 50% of all households living in 'shared' dwellings in 1966, the second highest rate in London; more households, therefore, live in small accommodation units of 1–3 rooms. (41.4% compared with 22.8% in Greater London). Tenure patterns are also distinctive. The private rented sector is exceptionally large (63% of households rent privately, compared with 37% in Greater London) and is let principally in the form of unfurnished accommodation (47%), althoug the furnished sector is also relatively large (17%). Housing in Hammersmith has one of the lowest amenity levels in London; only 42% of households have sole use of hot water, fixed bath and w.c., 25% of households have no bath at all. Amenity deficiency is highest in multi-occupied dwellings, both in terms of sharing and in total amenity lack. Eight wards in Hammersmith are calculated to be areas of severe housing pressure and fall within the worst 10% of wards from a housing point of view in Greater London.

Hammersmith is more difficult to characterise as a distinctive urban area than Coventry. It is very much an arbitrarily designated part of inner London, sharing both the wide range of employment opportunities and the problems of change and decline which are affecting the central areas of the capital. Its unemployment situation is generally good, but the economic changes in its area must be unsettling and sources of problems for some individuals.

Newcastle

Newcastle, a city of just over 220,000 people, is located in an area which has typically been considered as a 'problem region', when viewed in relation to the rest of the country. The mark of a 'problem region' in an economic sense is a level of unemployment consistently above the national average, and an economic structure which is heavily dependent on declining or stagnant industry. In the early 1960s the North East was identified as an area requiring special attention and the strategy advocated was one of diversifying the industrial structure plus 'positive action to improve the whole range of services which underpin the region's economic activity'. (HMSO, The North East). The activity was to be 'concentrated on that part of the region which has the most favourable conditions for self sustaining growth and is best placed to generate increased activity'. (*Ibid.*) Among the growth zones identified was Tyneside; the measures advocated to develop these zones were direct incentives to enterprise to come to the region, special attention to improving communications within the region and between the region and the rest of the country, accelerated investment and town-centre development. These policies were of course undertaken in the context of a whole battery of government policies in the form of grants, loans and inducements designed to tackle the problem of regional imbalance.

Whilst it is not possible to quantify precisely the benefit to regions that are recipients of aid, and there is plenty of scope for argument about the criteria of success for regional policy, Newcastle has undoubtedly benefited to some extent from some or all of these policies. Certainly it has attempted to establish itself as a 'regional capital' and since the mid-sixties quite extensive efforts have been made to redevelop the city, with a greater emphasis on service industries like banking, insurance and professional services than had been the case in earlier years. The wholesale reconstruction and rebuilding of the city centre is very much in evidence and whilst Newcastle might not yet be the 'Brasilia of the Old World' as some of its planners and politicians might wish (a view quoted by J. Gower Davies, p. 2), it is certainly not a city that fits easily into the stereotype of a depressed industrial area.

It would be complacent to suggest that central area redevelopment heralds a new era for Newcastle, but it is probably true that whilst the current economic recession has hit the north east hard, not all of the north east has suffered equally; and Newcastle has not suffered as much as some of the surrounding areas in terms of the rate of unemployment or the growth of the local economy. It it were possible to compute a current unemployment rate for Newcastle it would no doubt occupy a mid-point between that of the northern region and the figure for Great Britain. Certainly in the period when it was possible to calculate an unemployment rate for Newcastle this proposition held. Table 2.5 demonstrates this for 1963, the last year in which separate rates were calculated for Newcastle.

Table 2.5.   Unemployment rates 1963

	Newcastle	Northern Region	G.B.
January	5.1	6.5	3.6
February	5.5	7.1	3.9
March	5.1	6.0	3.1
April	4.2	5.1	2.7

Source: Ministry of Labour Gazette 1963

The preceding discussion has attempted to indicate that one should be chary of accepting too completely the traditional stereotype of Newcastle as a depressed town. Certainly some sectors of the Newcastle employment market have suffered from the traditional shortcomings of being dependent on industries that are declining in terms of their ability to absorb labour, but such a tendency has been offset by the introduction of growth-oriented industries as part of the regional strategy. One measure of the degree to which the balance of industry differs between areas is to look at the location quotients of industrial groups. The location quotient for any particular industry is the proportion employed in that industry in Newcastle, divided by the corresponding proportion in the area with which it is being compared. Such an exercise conducted for the period 1966–9 for Newcastle compared with the Northern Region reveals the extent to which the Newcastle industrial structure has become service industry oriented. Apart from the continued importance, but in reduced proportions, of traditional industries such as mechanical and marine engineering and shipbuilding, there is a marked rise in employment in service industries. Employment in service industries such as insurance, banking, finance, public administration is 28% above the regional average.

Taken overall, the pattern of employment in Newcastle differs from that of the region in the following respects:

(i)   The service sector is proportionately greater; in 1970, 71% of the total labour force in Newcastle was engaged in service industries.

(ii)   Manufacturing industry as a whole is of diminishing importance in Newcastle compared with the region; of those working in manufacturing employment 80% were concentrated in four industrial groups, namely engineering food, drink and tobacco; shipbuilding and marine engineering; and chemical and allied trades.

(iii)   Primary and extractive industries are of negligible importance.

Whilst it has been seen that as a result of the strategy of the last few years the service sector is in the ascendency as a major source of employment, there has in fact been an absolute decline in the work forces of all the industry groups taken together. In the five years 1965–70 employment in the city fell 9% whilst regional total employment increased by about 1½%. The population of the city fell over approximately the same period; the inter-censal decline being 1961: 269,678–1971: 222,153.

So far general trends of the employment situation in Newcastle have been discussed, but the extent to which such trends necessarily pattern the employment prospects of people must also be examined.

The first thing to note is that Newcastle is an employment magnet for towns surrounding it. The 1966 Census workplace movement tables show that there is considerable movement in and out of Newcastle for employment. Newcastle is the major outside employment centre for eight of the eleven residential authorities in the Tyneside conurbation, and the bulk of this inward movement represents white collar workers, employed in the service sector. This indicates that the beneficiaries of the new employment opportunities in Newcastle are not necessarily those living in Newcastle. In addition the rise in female

32

employment rates which has accompanied the rise in service sector employment would indicate that women have benefited more than men from the rise of employment in service industries. The rise in female employment rates has been such that the figures projected for female employees in the 1963 Development Plan Review of 38.40% for 1981 had been surpassed by 1971.

Whilst the expanding areas of employment have largely benefited women and those who commute to Newcastle for employment, the industries shedding labour largely employ men who live within the Newcastle area. Shipbuilding and engineering have both reduced their labour forces under the pressures of rationalisation and re-grouping. The Geddes Committee in 1967 (HMSO: *Shipbuilding Inquiry Committee 1965–66*) urged the concentration of the main strength of the shipbuilding industry in at least four groups; one of these groups has been the Tyneside Consortium, bringing together Swan Hunter at Wallsend, Redheads, Hawthorn Leslies and Vickers. The trend to amalgamation has also been evident in engineering, with the merger of Reyrolle and C.A. Parsons to form a holding company Reyrolle Parsons Ltd., comprising the largest engineering complex in the North East with a payroll of about 22,000.

Rationalisation in the traditional industries has been accompanied by technological change. This in turn has had an impact on the nature and quantity of the labour demand in these industries. It is difficult to quantify precisely the effects of these changes on the demand for labour, but a recent study of three labour forces in North East England illustrates (North East Development Council 1970) the way in which the various categories of labour are differently influenced by downturns in the overall demand for labour. In the shipbuilding industry on Tyneside the highest unemployment is amongst the old skills of joiners, ships' painters, polishers and others whose skills are intricate but not of much importance in the large scale work of, for example, tanker building. On the other hand the skills of platers, welders and shipwrights are at a premium. This is reflected in the unemployment rate in the industry. The unemployment rate of the skilled labour force (defined as having served a full apprenticeship) in shipbuilding for 1970 for the whole of the north east was 2.5% and the rates for the various skilled trades expressed as a percentage of skilled men unemployed in the industry were polishers 16%, marine engine fitters 14%, painters 7%, joiners 6%. Whilst well over 2,000 jobs have been lost in the Walker shipyard at Wallsend since the mid-1960s, not all sections of the labour force have been equally affected. The burden of unemployment is largely felt by those men who are either unskilled or have redundant skills.

The change in industrial structure and the rationalisation of the traditional industries have been accompanied by geographical dislocation for some workers. Re-organisation has meant for many workers an increase in the distance which they have to travel to work. A journey to work which previously involved a few minutes walk to the factory or shipyard may now involve a cross-town journey, which can be difficult since the public transport system has not kept pace with shifts in the location of residence in relation to work. Workers in the traditional industries have been used to short journeys to work and this in turn has created an expectation that they will not have to travel far to work. Coupled with the changes of location for work within the city have been the effects of siting new manufacturing industries on trading estates outside Newcastle.

Wages probably reflect the average for the industrial north east for male manual workers; £28.8 gross per week, with £35 for non-manual workers in April 1971. The average for all male workers was £30.8.

The employment and industrial aspects of Newcastle have been described briefly; it is now necessary to look at the social fabric of the city. The best that can be done is to provide a 'snap-shot' impression of the city as it appeared in the mid or late sixties, whilst noting that there is certain evidence of an attempt to change the city quite radically. Whether the physical changes will involve social change on an equally dramatic scale remains to be seen.

Newcastle's resident population examined in terms of the Registrar General's socio-economic groups contains a low proportion of executive and professional workers and a higher proportion of manual workers than do England and Wales as a whole. In 1966 12.2% of the economically active and retired males aged 15 and over were professional workers or employers and managers, whilst the figures for England and Wales were 18.7%. Skilled and unskilled manual workers account for 52% of the male working population in Newcastle, compared with 40% in England and Wales.

If it is accepted that such distinctions are based on groupings which are homogeneous in respect of the level of living, educational background and community interest, then Newcastle is in many respects a 'working class' town. Some areas of the city demonstrate the social cohesion and community of interest typically associated with the traditional working class community. Particularly this is so with regard to the inner east and west ends of the residential areas. These communities are, however, being eroded by the physical redevelopment of these areas, and have become, particularly in the west end, 'twilight zones', occupied by an increasingly transient population, many of whom might be described as 'deviants' forming a sub-culture of their own. Whether such areas merit the notoriety ascribed to them is a matter for debate. (See J. Gower Davies) As in other cities the outer areas consist of a mixture of middle class housing and new local authority estates, used to house those displaced by slum clearance.

The quality of the housing stock may well have been dramatically influenced by this new building. Hitherto the housing stock of Newcastle had been criticised as containing a large number of dwellings, small in size, having inadequate facilities and being generally outmoded in relation to 'present day' use. The 1966 Census revealed that a greater proportion of households in Newcastle were deficient in terms of at least one amenity compared with either the Tyneside conurbation or England and Wales.

In Newcastle 66.7% of households had exclusive use of hot water, fixed bath and inside w.c., compared with 70% for Tyneside and 72.4% for England and Wales as a whole.

Much of the new building of houses in Newcastle has been by the local authority and the housing stock is becoming increasingly local authority dominated. In 1966 the analysis of dwellings by tenure showed that 28% of the dwellings were owner occupied, 35% of the dwellings were rented from the local authority, and 32% of the dwellings were rented unfurnished from private persons. This represents a ratio of private to local authority housing of 40:60.

Newcastle, then, is very much a town of transition. The official policy is to throw off the image of the depressed area and assume the role of a 'regional capital'. Whether the resident population approves of such a change is a matter for conjecture. This change in emphasis has in part been responsible for the change in employment structure, but we must not ignore the effects of technological change and re-organisation in the traditional industries. Even allowing for change, the town still carries with it the spectre of the 1930s in so far as unemployment is concerned. Absolutely the problem may not be as grave, but the relative position is not necessarily mitigated for the unemployed by a new town centre or technological change.

The Samples

To provide a link between the profiles of the areas set out in this chapter and the analyses given in the next few chapters it is proposed here to describe the basic characteristics of the three samples. This discussion will be very brief, to give the reader a general introduction to the subsequent analyses; the details on which it is based will be found in the later chapters.

Although the main sources of information were interviews, wherever possible this was supplemented by data from official records. Thus the men's work and unemployment records held by the Employment Exchanges were examined. So too were their records of claims for sickness benefit. Finally, the Criminal Records Office supplied some information on all those convicted of crimes. Appendix I gives further information on the methodology of the study, including the measures adopted to preserve the privacy of the respondents.

The age distributions of the samples were very much as expected from an

examination of Department of Employment statistics, with both the young
and the elderly appearing prominently amongst the unemployed. Newcastle
was a slight exception to this with a low percentage of over sixties. However,
this finding was checked against the Department of Employment statistics
for that area, which show a similar if slightly less marked shortfall in this age
group. To some extent the elderly may have been rehoused outside the city
boundaries, but perhaps a more important factor to mention is the high
mortality and morbidity rates amongst working class men in the North East
(see Howe). Additionally it is important to bear in mind that elderly men with
exceptionally poor job prospects and an exhausted entitlement to unemployment benefit may more readily than others accept transfer to the sick list or
even remove themselves from any register of the Welfare State.

In Newcastle 95% of the sample were British born, and in fact the great
majority of these had been born in the North East of England. There were
significant numbers of immigrants from the Commonwealth and from Eire
in the samples from the other two areas, so that the British born only comprised
two-thirds of the Hammersmith sample and three-quarters of the Coventry one.
There were very few European immigrants in the samples. Both Coventry and
Hammersmith also had many British born who had moved away from the area
of their birth.

In all areas a little over half the samples were married, with Hammersmith
containing the highest proportion of single men and Newcastle the lowest.
According to the 1971 census 73% of the economically active males (that is
men in work or seeking work) in Coventry were married. In the Coventry
sample 56% were married. The census figure for Hammersmith was 61%
married, the sample figure was 51%. In Newcastle the census found 68% of
economically active males married, in the sample only 59% were married. So
in each area the single were over-represented amongst the unemployed.

Very few of the men in the samples had had much more than the minimum
education. The Newcastle sample were the worst educated with 91% having
no school qualifications, while the Hammersmith group were the most qualified
(74% with no qualifications). In each area only about 15% had any further
education qualifications. Graduates were rare, 5 in Coventry, 11 in Hammersmith and 4 in Newcastle. The figures obtained on school leaving ages suggested
that the samples had had slightly less schooling than the adult populations in
their areas, but precise comparisons are difficult to make.

In each area over fifty per cent were registered at the Employment Exchanges
as unskilled or semi-skilled workers. The Hammersmith sample had the fewest
in these categories (53%), and the Newcastle sample had the most (72%). In
Hammersmith there was a substantial group who were registered for non-manual
work, 27%; people of this kind were very rare in the other two areas. In
36

Coventry, on the other hand, skilled manual workers were relatively common (32%), whereas they comprised only about 20% of the samples in the other two areas. All three samples were markedly less skilled than the working population in their areas.

When the sample was drawn up on 1 October 1971, about half of the men in Coventry and Hammersmith had been out of work under three months and only about 10% over a year. In Newcastle, on the other hand, only just over a third had been out under three months while nearly a third had been unemployed over a year. In all three areas a high proportion were to remain out of work for the whole of the six months follow up period, because general employment prospects were very poor during that time. Naturally, the Newcastle sample fared the worst over this period while the Hammersmith group did best.

Nearly all the men in the samples who had been out of work more than four weeks had some form of social security income. In Coventry and Hammersmith around two-thirds were receiving unemployment benefit on 1 October 1971. In Newcastle, due to the fact that men who are out of work for long periods exhaust their entitlements to unemployment benefit, only about half were getting income from this source. Consequently supplementary benefit was more important as a source of income in that area, two-thirds being in receipt of it as against around 40% who were getting it in the other areas. In each area around 20% were getting both types of benefit.

The average weekly earnings for all males in the regions in which the three areas belong were earlier quoted as £33.8 in the West Midlands, £38 in London and £30.8 in the North, with manual workers earning rather more than non-manual workers in the West Midlands and rather less in the other two areas. The men in the unemployed samples were asked about their take home pay in their last jobs. While it is difficult to make a comparison between the net earnings quoted by the men and the gross earnings quoted by the Department of Employment survey, it is clear that the majority of the unemployed men had been getting earnings well below the regional averages. In Coventry and Hammersmith only about 20% had been getting over £30 per week, and about another 20% over £25. In Newcastle only 13% had got over £30 and only 14% between £25 and £30.

The housing conditions of the unemployed men were slightly better than those the 1966 census found for the populations of the areas, largely because a higher proportion of the unemployed were local authority tenants.

The details set out in this section can be summarised as follows. In all areas the unemployed tended to be either elderly or comparatively young, with little education and low skills. The single were over-represented, and although the men were predominantly British born there were significant numbers from the Black Commonwealth and from Eire in Coventry and Hammersmith. They tended to have been poorly paid in their last jobs, dependent at the time of interview upon either unemployment or supplementary benefit, and sometimes both, and unemployed in very many cases for less than three months, but likely to have difficulty in getting work in the next six months.

Newcastle presented the main exceptions to this picture, with rather fewer very elderly men, very many indeed with minimal education and skills, very few immigrants, very few with high earnings in their last jobs, and many who had been out of work a considerable while.

Hammersmith deviated in largely opposite directions, with rather more people with educational qualifications, a significant number of non-manual workers and the largest number of immigrants.

The Coventry sample was notable for the greater representation of skilled workers, but otherwise differed little from the picture given above.

3 The main determinants of unemployment length

Introduction

The preceding section outlined the main characteristics of the unemployed and placed them in the context of the areas in which the samples were drawn. In this chapter their characteristics are discussed in relation to the extent of unemployment in the current spell, the aim being to establish the most important determinants of unemployment length. Throughout, the intention has been to avoid any absolute definition of 'long-term' as against 'short-term' unemployment, but rather to show how certain key variables are associated with a gradation of unemployment lengths.

Data sources and the period studied

The indicators of unemployment which are most commonly referred to in this and subsequent chapters are based on material extracted from Employment Exchange records. A three year period (1 October 1968 to 1 October 1971) was selected for study and the number and the length of unemployment spells experienced by respondents during this time recorded. In addition, the starting date of the current spell of unemployment was noted and a six month follow up period allowed, at the end of which the proportion of men who had found work or who were no longer signing the register was calculated.

The standard three year period was additionally used for recording information on health (from records kept by local Department of Health and Social Security offices) and to some extent on criminality (from the Criminal Records Office). The choice of period was dictated partly by practical considerations (for instance records on employment tended to be inadequate for over three years back) and partly because the respondent's *recent* history was thought to be most relevant to his present position and prospects. It was recognised that the period studied occurred at an arbitrary point in a man's career and was not necessarily representative of his history as a whole. However, as more general questions on health, unemployment and reasons for unemployment were asked in the interview, it was hoped that the combination of both methods would not result in an unduly distorted picture.

Unemployment lengths

At the time they were selected for interview, the men had been unemployed for the lengths of time set out in Table 3.1.

Table 3.1.　Lengths of unemployment of men in the sample by 1 October 1971 (with percentages of totals in brackets)

	Coventry	Hammersmith	Newcastle
Under 3 months	178 (48)	128 (56)	141 (35)
3–6 months	78 (21)	45 (20)	78 (19)
6–9 months	48 (13)	19 (8)	44 (11)
9–12 months	26 (7)	15 (7)	24 (6)
Over 12 months	42 (11)	22 (10)	119 (29)
Total	372	229*	406*

(Note: *There were three men in Hammersmith and eight in Newcastle for whom information was not available on unemployment length)

As reported above, these men were followed up for six months to provide a more satisfactory measure of their unemployment length. These six months proved to be a very difficult time for men seeking work, 49% of the Coventry sample, 38% of the Hammersmith sample and 64% of the Newcastle sample remaining out of work for the whole six months.

To arrive at the measure of 'unemployment length' used in this book the unemployment lengths reported in Table 3.1 and any continuing unemployment in the six months follow-up period were added together for each man. The resultant 'lengths' for the samples are summarised in Table 3.2.

Table 3.2.　Percentages with various unemployment lengths

	Under 6 mths	6–12 mths	12–18 mths	18–24 mths	Over 24 mths
Coventry	29	45	16	3	7
Hammersmith	40	40	11	3	6
Newcastle	20	38	14	6	22

The mean unemployment lengths were 41.8 weeks in Coventry, 36.8 weeks in Hammersmith and 66.4 weeks in Newcastle. In the following discussion, when the relationship between specific variables and unemployment length is considered the latter expression must be taken to mean unemployment before 1 October 1971 (subject to a maximum of 3 years) plus unemployment after 1 October 1971 (subject to a maximum of 6 months).

Age

Table 3.3 shows that both the young and the elderly were prominent in the samples.

The under 25s figure markedly amongst the unemployed, even when, as here, the count is based upon a cross section of the 'register'. In view of the fact that they are rarely unemployed for very long they would be even more significant in a sample of newly unemployed in any particular period.

Table 3.3.   Numbers in each age group (with percentages in brackets)

	Coventry	Hammersmith	Newcastle
18–19	37 (10)	11 (5)	26 (6)
20–4	67 (18)	36 (16)	77 (19)
25–9	38 (10)	24 (10)	43 (11)
30–4	26 (7)	29 (13)	38 (9)
35–9	27 (7)	12 (5)	31 (8)
40–4	31 (8)	13 (6)	35 (9)
45–9	31 (8)	20 (9)	47 (12)
50–4	19 (5)	14 (7)	40 (10)
55–9	22 (6)	26 (11)	34 (8)
60+	74 (20)	44 (20)	37 (9)

Of all the factors which are considered in this book age is the most significant in relation to length of unemployment. Furthermore it was also associated with most of the other major factors to be discussed. Not surprisingly, the amount of sickness and disablement were linked with age, but it is also important to note that the elderly unemployed tended to be slightly less skilled and less well educated than the young unemployed. In many of the following sections, therefore, data will be presented in relation to age groups with the samples cut up into 3 age groups (under 25, 25–49, 50 and over). Table 3.4 gives a general indication of the strength of the relationship between age and

41

length of unemployment. In all three areas chi square tests of statistical significance[1] on the association between age cohorts and unemployment lengths provide results that are 'significant' above the 1% level. Although there appear to be some odd bulges in the distribution in Table 3.4 (amongst the 40—4s in Coventry for example), these are unlikely to have any special significance and may be attributed to sampling error.

Table 3.4.   Mean length of unemployment in weeks in each age group

	Coventry	Hammersmith	Newcastle
18—24	30.5	17.8	40.7
25—9	33.3	29.2	45.2
30—4	33.5	26.6	52.8
35—9	30.0	26.8	57.3
40—4	50.8	35.5	76.0
45—9	39.6	30.5	76.7
50—4	49.2	50.0	85.6
55—9	59.9	45.6	107.0
60+	59.3	64.4	103.6

In general these findings on age are closely similar to those in other studies of unemployment. In the United States the young figure prominantly amongst the unemployed, but not to the same extent amongst the long-term unemployed (J.M. Becker ed., chapters 2 and 3). The British studies of redundancy (Wedderburn; Kahn; Acton Society Trust) have also commented on the way employment problems increase with age. Sobel and Wilcock summarise the evidence, from a large number of countries, as follows:

All available statistics confirm the much longer duration of unemployment for workers over 45. In fact for every age group over 25, the average length of unemployment mounts with age.

Sinfield (O.E.C.D. 1968, p. 15) particularly stresses the fact that long-term unemployment increases sharply in the 5 to 10 years before the usual retirement age. However, he also points out that some evidence from the United

---

1 Readers unfamiliar with the concept of statistical significance should refer to the paragraph at the end of the methodological appendix.

States and Canada suggests that new entrants to the labour market are also vulnerable to long unemployment. The only British study to hint at the emergence of a similar problem was Gittus' study of Merseyside (in Lawton ed.), where high rates of long-term unemployment amongst the under 40s were found in the central Liverpool area. Despite the fact that our study was conducted in three highly urbanised areas, two of which (Newcastle and Hammersmith) have some characteristics in common with Central Liverpool, no comparable phenomenon was found.

Health

Evidence on the health of the men in the samples came from two sources, the men's own accounts of their health, disabilities and fitness for work, and the records of claims for sickness benefit kept by the Department of Health and Social Security. Some degree of association was found between the measures of fitness derived from these two sources, for example a positive relationship between weeks of sickness and whether or not the men claimed to be disabled was statistically significant above the 1% level in all three areas.

Only very small numbers in the three samples claimed to be actually unfit for work at the time of the interview (8 men in Coventry, 8 in Hammersmith, and 27 in Newcastle). Those that did so certainly experienced longer spells of unemployment than the others, 29 of them having unemployment lengths of over a year.

Similarly, comparatively few said they were receiving medical treatment (27 in Coventry, 20 in Hammersmith and 37 in Newcastle). No statistically significant relationship was found between this and unemployment length, in any area or in any of the three age groups in each area. By contrast, reported disablement seemed to be highly related to unemployment length. This was, of course, a subjective measure, but then all measures of disablement (including those arrived at by medical examinations) contain an element of 'opinion' on someone's part. The fact that the only measure of major importance for the present study was derived from a question 'Do you have any condition which you or others might consider a physical or mental disability?' should be treated with caution. However it was followed up by detailed questions about the disability, and will be shown to be a good predictor of unemployment length for various groups in the samples, so it should not be undervalued. Table 3.5 provides some basic information on numbers who said they were disabled, and the main disabilities mentioned are set out in Table 3.6. In the latter table only the commonest groups of disabilities mentioned are listed, and the percentages of the disabled accounted for are given at the end of the table.

43

The puzzling differences between the numbers disabled in Coventry and the other two areas will be related to other differences between the areas and discussed later in the book.

There is a highly statistically significant relationship (over the 1% level in all three areas) between reported disability and unemployment length. There is also an association, statistically significant at the 5% level in Coventry and Hammersmith and quite strong in Newcastle, between registration (with the Department of Employment) as disabled and unemployment length; however, there is a strong relationship here between this and age, so that the association is not statistically significant for any individual age group.

Most of those saying they were disabled were in the older age groups. In each area they were an insignificant proportion of the under 25s (6 men in Coventry, 4 in Hammersmith and 5 in Newcastle). In Coventry, about 26% of the 25–49 age group and about 29% of the over 50s said they were disabled. The percentages of disabled in those two age groups in Hammersmith were 13 and 50, and in Newcastle 25 and 50.

As a result of the importance of the age factor the associations between reported disability and unemployment length were, as was the case with registered disability, not very clear within the various age groups. Statistically significant associations at the 5% level were found for the under 25s and the over 50s in Hammersmith, and at the 1% level for the 25–49s in Newcastle. The figures for the two older age groups are set out in Table 3.7.

Table 3.5.   The Disabled–numbers (with percentages of the samples in brackets)

	Coventry	Hammersmith	Newcastle
Saying they were disabled (registered)	32 (9)	40 (17)	61 (15)
Saying disabled, but not registered	48 (13)	23 (10)	53 (13)
Total disabled	80 (22)	63 (27)	114 (28)

These figures show a tendency towards a relationship between unemployment length and possession of a disability for the over 50s in all areas, even though the relationship is only statistically significant in Hammersmith. The picture for the 25–49s is less clear except in the area where jobs are hard to get, Newcastle.

44

Table 3.6. Main Disability Types (with percentages of the total disabled in brackets)

	Coventry	Hammersmith	Newcastle
Mental disorders	10 (13)	11 (18)	13 (12)
Diseases of the nervous system	10 (13)	10 (16)	8 (7)
Diseases of bones & organs of movement	12 (15)	19 (15)	21 (19)
Bronchitis	6 (8)	6 (10)	16 (14)
Diseases of the digestive system	3 (4)	0 (–)	10 (9)
Multiple disabilities	7 (9)	8 (13)	26 (23)
Total of the disabled accounted for	48 (60)	44 (71)	94 (84)

Table 3.7. Numbers disabled by unemployment length (with percentages of total in that age and unemployment length group in brackets)

	Under 6 months	6 months to a year	Over a year
Age 25–49			
Coventry	10 (18)	17 (27)	12 (34)
Hammersmith	6 (14)	7 (13)	1 (17)
Newcastle	4 (11)	12 (15)	32 (43)
Age 50+			
Coventry	2 (14)	14 (25)	19 (38)
Hammersmith	4 (22)	16 (50)	24 (62)
Newcastle	2 (22)	17 (51)	40 (48)

Those who said they were disabled, but not registered as such with the Department of Employment, were asked if they had applied for registration. Very few had (12 in all areas together) and their reasons for failing to get registered were not very revealing. Those who had never applied were asked why not. Twenty-nine of the 68 codable replies were that they did not consider themselves sufficiently disabled. Only 4 said they did not know they could apply, and 3 that they did not think it helpful to register, and only 2 objected to the administrative or medical procedures involved, but 13 (8 of them in Newcastle) said they thought registration would limit their job opportunities. This last finding is similar to Sinfield's finding (1970, p. 226) that:

> Some of the disabled said they had refused to go on the Disabled Person's Register as they believed this hampered them in competing in the open market and encouraged employers to consider them only for lower paid jobs.

Over half of all those claiming to be disabled said that their disability had forced a change of occupation (55% in Coventry, 34% in Hammersmith, and 58% in Newcastle), but for many of them the main change was one of work environment rather than a change to a less skilled or less well paid job. Table 3.8 sets out the main changes quoted by respondents.

Table 3.8.   Percentages of those changing occupation giving various main kinds of change

	Coventry	Hammersmith	Newcastle
Change in work environment or conditions of work	33	27	45
Change from manual to non-manual	22	17	9
Change to less skilled work	16	17	9
Change to less well paid work	4	13	9
Change to light work	4	10	11
Other answers	21	16	17

There was a slight, but not statistically significant, tendency for those who said they had had to change their occupation to figure more in the ranks of the long-term unemployed than those amongst the disabled who had not had to change.

In Coventry 40% of those saying they were disabled were having treatment for their disability. Comparable figures for Hammersmith and Newcastle were 59% and 31% respectively. The individuals in these groups showed no tendency to experience longer unemployment than those amongst the disabled not receiving treatment. Clearly the wide range of disabilities involved here included some for which no current treatment was possible or appropriate, so that this

46

attempt to discover a measure of disability somewhat 'harder' than the subjective one derived by asking men whether they were disabled, was unsuccessful.

In each area a substantial proportion of the 'self-ascribed' disabled said they considered that their disability limited their chances of getting work (73% in Coventry, 79% in Hammersmith, and 84% in Newcastle). Their actual experience of unemployment supported their judgement. In two of the three areas, Coventry and Newcastle, those who said their disability limited their chances fared significantly worse than the rest of the disabled; and the disabled were, as has been shown, a markedly disadvantaged class as a whole.

Those who said their job chances were limited were asked how, and up to three ways were coded. In Table 3.9 these three ways are amalgamated regardless of the order in which they were originally mentioned. The other category is rather large when all three reasons are put together, but most of the main ways are set out in the table and the 'others' are a very varied bunch of second and third ways.

Table 3.9. Ways in which job chances are limited for the disabled (with percentages of the total saying their chances are limited, in brackets)

	Coventry ($N = 56$)	Hammersmith ($N = 48$)	Newcastle ($N = 84$)
Can only do light work	41 (73)	29 (60)	60 (71)
Can only do sheltered work	10 (18)	3 (6)	14 (17)
Employers discriminate	16 (29)	23 (48)	24 (29)
Can only work limited number of hours	9 (16)	5 (10)	9 (11)
Unable to use public transport	3 (5)	2 (4)	2 (2)
Others	9 (16)	19 (40)	28 (33)

The evidence quoted above, on which men had changed their occupations, suggested one of the reasons for the association between unemployment length and possession of a disability. This is supported by the fact that, in all three areas, a larger proportion of those registered at the Employment Exchanges for jobs of a semi-skilled or unskilled nature were disabled than those registered for skilled or non-manual jobs. This relationship is statistically significant in Coventry and Hammersmith and nearly so in Newcastle. Equally very few of the men who said they could only do non-manual work (2 in Coventry and 2 in Newcastle) were in fact registered for such work. In general this evidence leads to a conclusion similar to that adopted by Sinfield in his study of North Shields (1970, p. 226), that very many of the disabled get registered as light labourers and that 'where men with skill or training were having to take jobs as labourers and the number registered for this occupation far exceeded vacancies, this classification seemed tantamount to "reject" '.

In general these findings support the findings of other studies on the significance of disabilities for unemployment. The association is fairly obvious and persists despite the many measures adopted to assist disabled workers. Its significance is more fully discussed in Sinfield's O.E.C.D. study *The Long-Term Unemployed* and Beatrice Reubens' *The Hard to Employ: European Programs.* In particular, other writers have stressed the devastating impact of advanced age and disability in combination, as Wedderburn put it 'even a full employment situation cannot deal with the twin handicaps of age and failing health'. (Wedderburn, 1965, p. 9). The findings from the present sources certainly confirm this. In Hammersmith 49% of the over 50s said they were disabled and 62% of those unemployed over a year gave this reply. Comparable figures for Coventry were 29% and 38%, and for Newcastle 49% and 52%.

From the examination of the records of sickness benefit claims two closely related indices of health were derived, spells of sickness in the previous three years and months of sickness in that period. The general findings for the three samples are set out in Tables 3.10 and 3.11.

Table 3.10.   Spells of sickness between 1 October 1968 and 30 September 1971 (percentages in brackets)

	Coventry	Hammersmith	Newcastle
0	109 (30)	65 (31)	148 (37)
1	81 (22)	56 (26)	77 (19)
2	65 (18)	35 (17)	54 (14)
3	32 (9)	22 (10)	32 (8)
4	19 (5)	12 (6)	21 (5)
5+	55 (15)	22 (10)	69 (17)

Months of sickness were not statistically significantly related to unemployment length in any area or with any of the three main age groups, but came

48

Table 3.11. Months of sickness between 1 October 1968 and 30 September 1971 (percentages in brackets)

	Coventry	Hammersmith	Newcastle
Under 3 months	274 (76)	165 (79)	310 (77)
3–6 months	47 (13)	20 (10)	48 (12)
6–9 months	21 (6)	10 (5)	19 (5)
9–12 months	8 (2)	4 (2)	9 (2)
Over 1 year	10 (3)	11 (5)	15 (4)

fairly close to being so and were strongly related to whether or not men were disabled. This variable was also related to the occupational level for which men were registered, with lower amounts of sickness amongst the non-manual and skilled workers. This relationship was above the 5% 'significance' level in Coventry and Hammersmith.

This absence of a statistically significant relationship between weeks of sickness and unemployment length is probably explained by a number of factors. First, the sickness records are inadequate for men whose insurance contribution records are so poor that they have no entitlement to sickness benefit. These men often cease to send certificates in, or only send them to the Supplementary Benefits Office, once it is established that they have no entitlement. The men in a sample of the unemployed who fall in this category will tend to be those who have had a great deal of unemployment. Second, it may often be the case that men who are unemployed and temporarily sick will not bother to shift from one register of the Welfare State to another, but will continue to sign at the Employment Exchange. Third, since both sickness and unemployment were being measured over a fixed period of time it must be the case that at very long durations sickness and unemployment are mutually exclusive.

These points are reinforced by the curious results from Newcastle where a strong statistically significant ($p = < .01$) relationship was found between spells of sickness and unemployment length, based upon an association between low sickness and low unemployment, high sickness and medium length unemployment (six months to a year), and low sickness and long unemployment. Here the 'long unemployment' group contains a considerable number of men who were unemployed throughout the three year period studied.

The general problem with evaluating information on health lies in choosing between a measure that is inadequate because it is subjective, which is inevitably related to unemployment because men will be very ready to explain employment

49

problems in terms of disabilities, and a measure whose limitations stem from the fact that it is derived from records kept for the purpose of the administration of an insurance scheme and not from any need to keep a complete and accurate record of men's health problems.

A similar problem has to be faced when mental health is examined. Here the insurance records provided merely evidence of spells of sickness during which men were certified by their doctors to be suffering from mental illnesses. Such illnesses ranged from 'nervous debility' to 'schizophrenia', involving varied and not necessarily accurate descriptions of complaints. They figured but rarely in the records, which is not surprising, and were therefore very little use for the present investigation. Only 13 men in Coventry, 25 in Hammersmith, and 11 in Newcastle had any spells of sickness attributed to mental illness. The larger number from the smallest sample, Hammersmith's, is deserving of a tentative note, though it cannot be related clearly to length of unemployment.

The alternative to the use of such inadequate records was to include in the questionnaire some means of measuring any tendencies towards mental illness. A short 20 item prediagnostic scale was used, the 'Personal Disturbance (P.D.) scale' from Foulds' 'Symptom Sign Inventory'. This scale could be used by lay interviewers. It was generally accepted by respondents, and was completed for most of the men, other than those whose interviews had to be translated into a foreign language. Men scoring 5 or more on this scale can be said to be likely to be suffering from some degree of mental illness. The results found by this technique are presented in Table 3.12 for each area and for three different unemployment lengths.

Table 3.12.   Numbers with P.D. scores of 5 and over (with percentages in brackets) by unemployment lengths

	0–6 months	6–12 months	Over 12 months
Coventry	15 (15)	33 (22)	22 (25)
Hammersmith	31 (35)	21 (23)	15 (35)
Newcastle	7 (9)	25 (16)	37 (23)

There is a statistically significant relationship between high P.D. score and long unemployment in Newcastle, and a tendency in the same direction in Coventry. But in Hammersmith, where as many as 30% of the whole sample scored over 5 (a figure that fits with the higher amounts of mental illness indicated by medical certificates), the relationship to unemployment length was an odd one, with a markedly lower number of high P.D. scorers with over

6 months but less than 12 months unemployment. Furthermore, as very few men had over 12 months unemployment in Hammersmith it is appropriate to amalgamate the figures for all lengths of over 6 months. This gives a percentage of only 27%.

The interpretation problem posed by these results is further confused when the results for different age groups are examined. In Coventry and Newcastle the same general direction was found for the association between P.D. scores and unemployment length, with a statistically significant association amongst the under 25s in Newcastle ($p = <.05$) and some signs of an association amongst the 25–49s in Coventry. In Hammersmith, however, there was a strong statistically significant ($p = <.01$) inverse relationship for the 25–49 group. In other words, those suspected of being mentally ill seem to have had a substantially better chance of getting back to work in Hammersmith than those presumed to be fully fit in this respect.

There is a general absence of statistically significant relationships between P.D. scores and education, occupation or age; the few solitary 'significant' chi squares being for a tendency for high P.D. scorers to be low skilled ($p = <.01$) and young ($p = <.05$) in Coventry and to have left school young ($p = <.05$) in Hammersmith. These findings do not help to explain the conflict between the Hammersmith findings and those for the other two areas, and it must therefore be observed, in concluding this discussion, that in some cases men were counted as no longer unemployed when they had become sick, been sent to prison, or just ceased to register as unemployed for no particular reason. The inclusion of this small group as 'back to work' does not have a distorting effect on large numbers but may upon certain specific subgroups. The mentally ill in Hammersmith, an area in which there is likely to be a tendency for such individuals to move around to other rooms and lodgings without at once making specific arrangements for their continued support, are one such sub-group. So too are men with convictions, for whom some rather surprising results are reported later. This supposition receives further support from the fact that for Hammersmith there is a statistically significant association ($p = <.05$) between P.D. score and the number of times the men reported being unemployed before. This tendency for men who acknowledged having had a large number of job changes to be high P.D. scorers suggests that in the good employment conditions prevailing in London a group of this kind will be more readily recognisable by their tendency to change jobs than by their tendency to remain unemployed. This is an issue that will be more fully explored in the second book on this research project.

Birthplaces

Not very surprisingly, Newcastle differed markedly from the other two areas in the extent to which its unemployed population included 'immigrants', both from elsewhere in the world and from elsewhere in the United Kingdom. 95% of the unemployed in that area were born in Britain, as opposed to 74% of the unemployed in Coventry and 66% in Hammersmith. Furthermore 66% of Newcastle's British born unemployed were born in the city and a further 23% in the Northern region (mainly in fact in Northumberland or County Durham). The findings on these points for all three areas are set out in Tables 3.13 and 3.14.

Table 3.13.   Countries of birth (percentages in brackets)

	Coventry	Hammersmith	Newcastle
Britain	276 (74)	153 (66)	390 (95)
Black Commonwealth	52 (14)	41 (18)	10 (2)
Eire	33 (9)	26 (11)	5 (1)
East Europe	10 (3)	6 (3)	5 (1)
Rest of the World	1 (0)	7 (3)	2 (0)

Table 3.14.   Birthplaces–British born (percentages in brackets)

	Coventry	Hammersmith	Newcastle
Survey Area	137 (50)	88 (58)	258 (66)
South East	13 (5)	11 (7)	8 (2)
Midlands	46 (16)	21 (14)	8 (2)
North-West and Yorkshire	18 (6)	6 (4)	10 (3)
North	7 (3)	0 (–)	91 (23)
Wales and South-West	14 (5)	12 (8)	3 (1)
Scotland	25 (9)	12 (8)	12 (3)
N. Ireland	16 (6)	3 (2)	0 (–)

The 'survey areas' in Table 3.14 are Coventry, the County of London and Newcastle respectively. The hypothesis that people who remain in the area in which they were born are more prone to long-term unemployment was tested; this received slight but not statistically significant support.

The numbers of Commonwealth immigrants amongst the unemployed in

Coventry and Hammersmith seemed rather higher than might be expected if their unemployment experience were no greater than that of the British born population. There is however extreme difficulty involved in estimating the percentage of immigrants in the work forces of these areas. In Chapter 2 estimates were quoted of 3.3% for the percentage in the Coventry population from the black Commonwealth and 8.0% for the percentage in Hammersmith, but (a) these figures were out of date and may well have been underestimated due to undernumeration in the census, and (b) while it may be presumed that there were many children and few elderly people in the immigrant numbers it is impossible to achieve anything better than a wild and misleading guess at the percentage in the work-force.

A more feasible question to ask in the context of this survey was 'Did the Commonwealth immigrants in the Coventry and Hammersmith samples experience longer unemployment than the non-immigrants?' No general evidence was found to support the view that Commonwealth immigrants had either significantly longer or significantly shorter unemployment than the other people in the sample.

Immigrants tend to be amongst the younger men in the sample, and this must have an impact upon the inconclusive results reported above. On the other hand they tend to be less skilled, and skill is another factor that will subsequently be shown to be related to unemployment length. It is therefore valid to compare the unemployment lengths of immigrants and non-immigrants when age and skill are taken into account. This is done in Table 3.15 with reference to low skilled men in the 25–49 age group, this being the only combined age/skill category within which a sizeable number of immigrants are found.

Table 3.15.   Men aged 25–49 and registered as semi- or unskilled workers by country of origin and length of unemployment (Black Commonwealth against all others) in Coventry and Hammersmith (percentages in brackets).

	Under 6 months	6 months to 1 year	Over 1 year
(1) Coventry			
Black Commonwealth	6 (21)	7 (17)	7 (25)
Others	22 (79)	35 (83)	21 (75)
(2) Hammersmith			
Black Commonwealth	4 (22)	10 (34)	1 (50)
Others	14 (78)	19 (66)	1 (50)

Table 3.15 indicates that immigrants from the Black Commonwealth in Hammersmith, but not in Coventry, are prone to longer spells of unemployment. It should be noted, here, that the immigrant group in Coventry is predominantly Asian, while in Hammersmith it is more mixed, with a slight preponderance of West Indians.

Marital Status and Family Commitments

56% in the Coventry sample, 51% of the Hammersmith sample and 59% of the Newcastle sample were married. These figures were not based upon 'legal' definitions of marriage; men were counted as married if they said so and also, to be consistent with this, if they told us they were living with 'common law' wives. Accordingly the numbers in the survey counted as 'separated, divorced or widowed' were a small and rather heterogeneous group, about whom it is difficult to generalise. They included only 10% of the samples in Coventry and Hammersmith and 12% in Newcastle.

There was a slight tendency for the married to experience longer unemployment than the single and for the 'others' to be out of work longer than either, but these figures must be related to age. The single were on the whole younger than the married and the 'others' tended to be the most elderly. When age was taken into account there was little difference between the 'statuses', with the exception that the elderly single seemed prone to longer unemployment. There was a statistically significant difference of this kind amongst the over 50s in Hammersmith. On the other hand the 'others' were more similar to the married than the single in their experience of long unemployment, when age was controlled.

Since men with several children tend to require higher social security incomes, which may often reduce the gap between what they can earn and the benefits they get when out of work to a very small amount, it was important to examine differences in family size and consider whether men with several children were prone to long unemployment. Table 3.16 shows the numbers of married men in the three samples with various numbers of dependent children.

Clearly there were quite substantial numbers in the samples with above-average sized families. The difficulty about comparing unemployment lengths of men with different numbers of children is that the most unemployment prone are the elderly, who often no longer have dependent children. So a comparison was made by breaking the sample into three age groups. This revealed no association, nor did a comparison taking the other factor likely to have a distorting effect—skill level—into account.

It can therefore be said that this study found no evidence to support a

54

Table 3.16. Numbers of dependent children—married men only (percentages in brackets)

	Coventry	Hammersmith	Newcastle
0	90 (45)	61 (53)	72 (30)
1	33 (16)	16 (14)	47 (20)
2	30 (15)	10 (9)	48 (20)
3	15 (7)	21 (18)	31 (13)
4+	34 (17)	8 (7)	42 (18)

finding from the Pilgrim Trust study in the Thirties:

> The birth-rate for Leicester is actually comparatively low, and yet of the men under 50 who were out of work no less than 11 of the 32 have families of five or more children. The conclusion is irresistable: that men who get a large unemployment allowance ... tend more than others to fall out of employment and "live on the dole!"

This kind of crude reasoning has entered into the folklore on unemployment. In the next chapter this subject will be followed up by references to the relationships between incomes in and out of work. Some rather different evidence will be discussed there and it will be shown that there are difficult problems of interpretation in relation to questions about low incentives to work. What is quite clear, however, is that there is no straightforward relationship between family size and proneness to long-term unemployment.

The men were asked about commitments to maintain wives and children living outside their household at the time of interview. There are two theories about such commitments, that they operate as a deterrent to working because they are likely to be enforced by the courts when men have earnings, or that they spur men to get work in order to meet their commitments as fully as possible. Unfortunately the numbers with such commitments were very low, making any proper test of such theories impossible. The available evidence tends to support the incentive rather than the deterrent theory. Of the 28 with such commitments in Coventry only 3 were out of work over a year; corresponding figures for Hammersmith were 10 and 1, and for Newcastle 22 and 3. The percentages in the whole samples with unemployment lengths over a year were 26% in Coventry, 21% in Hammersmith and 42% in Newcastle.

9 out of the 28 with commitments to dependents in Coventry had court orders to pay, 1 of the 10 in Hammersmith, and 17 of the 22 in Newcastle.

The remainder described their commitments as voluntary.

In addition to those with commitments to wives and/or children there were a further 21 in Coventry, 21 in Hammersmith and 4 in Newcastle who said they had commitments to other relatives, mostly in fact to parents.

Education

Two factors clearly related to unemployment were education and skill level. At the same time they were closely inter-related, and it therefore makes more sense to stress the impact of skill and occupational experience rather than education, when looking at unemployment amongst men of all ages, very many of whom completed their formal education a long while ago. If little is made of the evidence from this section when the findings are discussed later in the book, therefore, relative to the significance of the relationship between education and unemployment, it is because it is seen as a prelude to the important section that follows on occupational and skill levels.

Table 3.17 provides some information on the school leaving ages of the men in the three samples. The marked contrast between Newcastle and the other areas is to some degree a reflection of the lower skill levels of the men in that sample, but it must also be pointed out that the other samples included a substantial group of foreign-born men, some of whom left school above the British minimum age but did not necessarily have more years' schooling. In fact amongst the British born 80% in Coventry and 67% in Hammersmith left school at 15 or under.

It is also worth noting in connection with Table 3.17 that most children at schools for the educationally sub-normal stay there until they are 16.

Table 3.17.   School leaving ages (percentages in brackets)

	Coventry	Hammersmith	Newcastle
15 or under	282 (76)	145 (63)	360 (87)
16	58 (16)	37 (16)	29 (7)
17	12 (3)	15 (7)	9 (2)
18 or over	19 (5)	33 (14)	15 (4)

There was a strong statistically significant ($p = < .01$), association between school leaving age and length of unemployment in Coventry and Newcastle. It was partly a consequence of the fact that the more unemployment prone elderly had less schooling. Nevertheless when age was taken into account a statistically significant association was still apparent amongst under 25s in both areas, the 25–49s in Coventry and the over 50s in Newcastle.

On the assumption that the absence of a comparable set of relationships in Hammersmith might be due to the distorting effect of the foreign born, tests were carried out with this group excluded. This adjustment made very little difference in any area and Hammersmith's 'deviance' remained unexplained.

However in all three areas there is a statistically significant association ($p = <.01$) between school leaving age and registered occupation, so strong in fact that when occupation is taken into account there is no residual association between school leaving age and unemployment length. Very few people in the semi- and unskilled occupational groups had had more than the minimum education.

In the light of this information on school leaving ages and that to follow on qualifications, the findings on types of school attended are not very surprising. 61% of Coventry's sample, 47% of Hammersmith's and 82% of Newcastle's went to elementary or secondary-modern schools. Only 9% in Coventry, 14% in Hammersmith and 9% in Newcastle went to grammar schools. The remainder, apart from 9% who went to comprehensive schools in Coventry, mainly went to foreign schools, since very few went to British independent schools.

Table 3.18 sets out numbers and percentages in the three samples with qualifications of any kind when they left school.

Table 3.18. Educational qualifications on leaving school (with percentages in brackets)

	Coventry	Hammersmith	Newcastle
'A' level, Higher School Cert. etc.	12 (3)	16 (7)	13 (3)
'O' level, School Cert. etc.	31 (8)	22 (10)	17 (4)
R.S.A., C.S.E., City and Guilds	7 (2)	4 (2)	5 (1)
Others (mainly local low level qualifications)	15 (4)	4 (2)	1 (0)
Foreign qualifications	8 (2)	12 (5)	0 (–)
No qualifications	295 (80)	169 (74)	371 (91)

An examination of the relationship of these qualification levels to unemployment length and skill levels yields exactly the same results as did school leaving age, namely a very strong and statistically significant association between educational qualifications and occupations in all three areas, and a statistically significant association between qualifications and unemployment length in Newcastle and Coventry. The general nature of the latter association is set out clearly in Table 3.19. It shows that the Hammersmith figures run rather roughly in the same direction as those in the other two areas, even though the relationship is not statistically significant.

Table 3.19. Numbers of those in each unemployment length without school qualifications (with percentages in brackets)

	Under 6 months	6 months to a year	Over a year
Coventry	74 (68)	135 (83)	86 (90)
Hammersmith	64 (73)	66 (71)	39 (85)
Newcastle	61 (76)	138 (90)	172 (99)

An examination of further education qualifications reveals even fewer with these qualifications than with school ones. The basic findings are set out in Table 3.20.

It was hypothesized that illiteracy might be significant amongst the unemployed, and particularly amongst those out of work for a long while. 15% of the Coventry sample said they could not read or write very well and 5% said they could not read or write English at all. The figures for Hammersmith were 15% and 3% respectively, and for Newcastle 10% and 3%. The numbers and percentages of those with various unemployment lengths unable to read and write well are set out in Table 3.21.

The relationship between unemployment length and illiteracy was only statistically significant in Newcastle ($p = < .02$). Furthermore, when age was taken into account the level of statistical significance fell below acceptable levels for the three age groups used.

In the other areas it might be thought that the inclusion of a number of people born outside Britain was adding to the illiterates with relatively short unemployment lengths. This seems to have been the case, for in Coventry the percentages of the British in each of the unemployment lengths cited in Table 3.21 who were unable to read and write well were 5%, 15% and 12%. Comparable figures for Hammersmith were 7%, 13% and 21%. But these differences

58

Table 3.20.　Further educational qualifications

	Coventry	Hammersmith	Newcastle
Degree etc.	5	11	4
Higher National Cert. or Diploma	4	2	2
Teachers certificate, Membership of a professional institution, S.R.N.	3	2	1
G.C.E. A, Intermediate Arts/Sciences	1	0	1
Ordinary National Cert. or Diploma	5	1	1
G.C.E. O, School Certificate	3	1	3
City and Guilds, Forces Educational Certificates	24	6	31
Others	11	10	11
Total and % of sample	56 (15)	33 (14)	54 (13)

Table 3.21.　Numbers of those in each unemployment length unable to read and write well (with percentages in brackets)

	Under 6 months	6 months to 1 year	Over 1 year
Coventry	19 (18)	34 (21)	20 (20)
Hammersmith	14 (15)	15 (16)	35 (28)
Newcastle	4 (5)	16 (11)	32 (18)

between the proportions in the different unemployment lengths were not statistically significant.

Illiteracy was, not surprisingly, most statistically significantly related to occupational level ($p = < .01$). Yet, when the relationship between literacy and unemployment length was examined for each occupation group (with the foreign born excluded), the only 'significant' result was for unskilled workers in Coventry ($p = < .01$). The figures illustrating this association are set out in Table 3.22. They show some degree of association in each area, and also make clear that the 'significant' result in Coventry was one in which only the medium length unemployed in the group were markedly less literate. Perhaps age plays

59

a part here, as many of the long-term unemployed were elderly, so that the impact of age masked the impact of illiteracy. The numbers in the categories would be too low to allow a useful breakdown by age here.

Table 3.22. Numbers of those in each unemployment length unable to read and write well. British born workers registered as unskilled only (with percentages in brackets)

	Under 6 months	6 months to 1 year	Over 1 year
Coventry	1 (8)	15 (32)	7 (24)
Hammersmith	4 (24)	5 (28)	12 (21)
Newcastle	4 (15)	14 (18)	28 (21)

The men in the sample were asked if they had had any 'special schooling'. Very few replied in the affirmative to this question; 5% in Coventry, 9% in Hammersmith and 7% in Newcastle. Most of these had either been to an Approved School or a school for backward children.

A rather higher proportion said their schooling had been interrupted in some way; 19% in each area. There was a slight relationship between this and extent of unemployment, with those who had had their schooling interrupted figuring a little more amongst those with longer unemployment in all three areas. When the analysis of this question was confined to those who left school at 15 or below, a statistically significant relationship of this kind was found in Coventry ($p = < .05$) and one only just below the 5% level in Hammersmith.

In Coventry 75% of those who said their schooling had been interrupted said it was for less than one year, but in Hammersmith only 44% and in Newcastle only 48% said it had been for less than a year. There was no clear pattern of association between unemployment length and the extent to which schooling had been interrupted. The commonest reason given for the interruption of schooling was health. There was some association between this and unemployment length, for only 2 out of the 26 who gave this reason in Coventry, 6 out of 17 in Hammersmith and 6 out of 38 in Newcastle had unemployment lengths of under 6 months. Those reporting interruption of schooling were fairly evenly spread through the age groups but tended to be a little fewer amongst the elderly.

Occupation and skill levels

In Tables 3.23, 3.24 and 3.25 the skill distributions of the samples are set out using 3 different measures of skill, the occupations the men considered to be their 'usual' ones, their last jobs and the occupational registrations for them used by the Employment Exchanges. Though the 3 measures differ in the extent to which they provide evidence of skill, they all demonstrate the heavy impact of unemployment amongst the low skilled. The entry 'none' in the tables has been applied only to those saying they had no 'usual' occupation.

Table 3.23.   Skill levels—Coventry (percentages in brackets)

	Usual Job	Last Job	Registered Occupation
Registrar General's Classes			
1 and 2	24 (7)	18 (5)	14 (4)
3 non-manual	16 (4)	16 (5)	17 (5)
3 manual	164 (45)	144 (40)	117 (32)
4	90 (25)	105 (29)	83 (23)
5	65 (18)	76 (21)	132 (36)
None	3 (1)	–	–

Table 3.24.   Skill levels—Hammersmith (percentages in brackets)

	Usual Job	Last Job	Registered Occupation
Registrar General's Classes			
1 and 2	33 (15)	36 (16)	30 (13)
3 non-manual	23 (10)	22 (10)	31 (14)
3 manual	63 (28)	59 (26)	43 (19)
4	51 (23)	64 (29)	38 (17)
5	30 (13)	43 (19)	83 (37)
none	25 (11)	–	–

Table 3.25. Skill levels—Newcastle (percentages in brackets)

	Usual Job	Last Job	Registered Occupation
Registrar General's Classes			
1 and 2	16 (4)	15 (4)	10 (3)
3 non-manual	21 (5)	19 (5)	20 (5)
3 manual	159 (40)	126 (32)	82 (21)
4	69 (17)	102 (26)	36 (9)
5	121 (31)	130 (33)	251 (63)
none	11 (3)	—	—

It is very noticeable that the classification of men by what they declared to be their 'usual occupation' suggests that the sample was more highly qualified than the classification based upon the occupations for which the men were 'registered' by the Department of Employment. The classification of men according to their 'last job' places them somewhere between these two extremes.

To clarify further this apparent discrepancy it is helpful to relate last jobs to registered occupations. In Coventry 27 men were registered for occupations 'above' the level of their last job, whilst 92 were registered at levels below. Most significantly, 38% of the men whose last job was skilled were registered for semi-skilled or unskilled jobs. In Hammersmith 19 were registered 'above' their last job, and 71 below; there, 36% of those who had been skilled were registered as semi- or unskilled. The figures for Newcastle were 23 'above' their last job and 152 'below', with 44% of formerly skilled registered as semi- or unskilled.

Quite a number of the people whose last jobs were skilled, but who were not registered as skilled, said they were disabled (11 in Coventry, 6 in Hammersmith and 12 in Newcastle). These constituted about 40% of all the disabled men whose last jobs were skilled.

All three of the occupational level indices discussed above were associated to some degree with the length of unemployment, with usual occupation the least clearly associated and registered occupation the most clearly associated. This may be taken as some justification for the Employment Exchanges' perceptions of the degree of skill possessed by the men, or do their classifications create a self-fulfilling prophecy?

As might be guessed from the data on educational backgrounds discussed earlier, Hammersmith differed from the other two areas in that there was not a statistically significant relationship there between unemployment length and registered occupation. Indeed, none of the occupational measures was 'significantly' associated with unemployment length in that area. In Newcastle there was a strongly 'significant' association between registered occupation and unemployment length ($p = <.01$) and in Coventry there was a 'significant' one ($p = <.05$). It is worth noting that in Coventry alone there was a stronger association ($p = <.01$) between usual occupation and unemployment length than there was between registered occupation and length. Distributions for all three areas showing the relationship between registered occupation and unemployment length are set out in Table 3.26.

Table 3.26. Numbers of men of each unemployment length in each registered occupational category (with percentages in brackets)

| | Coventry | | |
	Under 6 months	6 months to 1 year	Over 1 year
Non-manual workers	11 (11)	14 (9)	6 (6)
RGs class 3 manual	39 (38)	52 (32)	26 (27)
RGs class 4	30 (29)	34 (21)	19 (20)
RGs class 5	23 (22)	63 (39)	46 (47)
	Hammersmith		
Non-manual workers	24 (27)	25 (27)	12 (26)
RGs class 3 manual	24 (27)	13 (14)	6 (13)
RGs class 4	10 (11)	19 (21)	9 (20)
RGs class 5	30 (34)	34 (37)	19 (41)
	Newcastle		
Non-manual workers	9 (12)	15 (10)	6 (4)
RGs class 3 manual	28 (37)	38 (25)	16 (9)
RGs class 4	9 (12)	17 (11)	10 (6)
RGs class 5	30 (39)	83 (54)	138 (81)

There was a slight association between registered occupation and age, statistically significant in Newcastle at the 5% level, nearly so in Coventry and Hammersmith. The elderly were more likely to be registered for low skilled work. Once the sample was divided into 3 age groups, a statistically significant

63

association ($p = < .05$) between unemployment length and registered occupation was, however, still found amongst the under 25s and 25–49s in Coventry, and amongst the 25–49s and the over 50s in Newcastle. The other groups in Coventry and Newcastle still showed some degree of association.

Low skill, advanced age and disability are the three factors which are almost universally stressed as associated with long-term unemployment (see Sinfield, O.E.C.D., 1968; Sinfield 1970; Franke in Becker ed.; Acton Society Trust; Bosanquet and Standing). Only Gittus' Merseyside study (Lawton ed.) differed from this conclusion 'For the registered occupation there is no evidence that the percentage classed as unskilled among the unemployed exceeded the expected figure based on the active labour force, and this holds regardless of the length of unemployment'.

It is interesting to note therefore that the area in the present study which is perhaps most comparable to inner Merseyside, Hammersmith, is one where similarly skill differences are relatively less important.

Sinfield (O.E.C.D. 1968) also commented that skill differentials are least marked 'with increasing or high levels of unemployment', and suggested a need to distinguish between a type of long-term unemployment resulting from permanent displacement 'due to plant closure or obsolescence of skill' and 'that associated with low skill, low wage and low security employment'. According to this line of argument, which admittedly Sinfield advanced very tentatively, the skill differential ought to be least significant in Coventry, whereas in fact it was most marked there.

Respondents were asked a number of questions designed to provide some idea of their occupational versatility. These questions provided ample evidence that these unemployed men had a great deal of varied work experience. Only 23% in Coventry, 19% in Hammersmith and 24% in Newcastle said that all their working life had been spent in one occupation. At the other extreme 12% in Coventry, 18% in Hammersmith and 11% in Newcastle said that they did not think of themselves as having 'one occupation in particular'. 59% of the Coventry sample had done three or more different kinds of work in their life. The corresponding figures for Hammersmith and Newcastle were 69% and 60%. The criteria used for distinguishing 'separate' occupations was that they had different code numbers in the Registrar General's classification scheme. This means that on the whole they were fairly distinctly different, tending to entail something more than doing the same kind of work in different environments.

The information acquired on the industries in which the men in the sample were last employed naturally reflects the occupational structures of their areas. It is reported in percentage form in Table 3.27.

There was relatively little difference between the groups with various unemployment lengths as far as their last industries were concerned. In Coventry men formerly employed in construction were slightly over-represented amongst the long-term. However, the workers in this category were predominantly low skilled (72% were semi- or unskilled). In Newcastle, on the other hand, workers in construction were under-represented amongst the long-term unemployed, while workers in manufacturing were over-represented. In this case their skill distributions were broadly similar, 71% in manufacturing and 77% in construction being semi- or unskilled. The association in this case was not significant. Neither of these associations was linked with age. On the other hand, the only industrial group in Hammersmith to stand out as over-represented amongst the long-term unemployed were men from the service sector who were markedly older than average.

Table 3.27.   Percentages whose last jobs were in various industrial groups

	Coventry	Hammersmith	Newcastle
Mining	1	0	2
Manufacturing	63	28	33
Construction	13	10	26
Transport	3	7	9
Distribution	6	14	7
Service and Public Administration	10	37	18
Unclear or not applicable (and agriculture—1% in Newcastle)	5	4	4

Crime

Information on the criminal records of men in the samples was obtained from the Criminal Records Office. These records do not, in general, contain evidence on very minor crimes, but there is neither certainty nor consistency on the part of those who prepare these records as to the exact point at which the line should be drawn between offences that should and should not be recorded.

The information obtained was analysed in total, and in relation to the period 1 October 1968 to 30 September 1971. It was considered appropriate to focus on the recent past since there are grounds for doubt about the relevance of a very old criminal record to the employment record of a man today.

As general indices of criminality two alternative measures were tried, number of convictions and number of separate occasions on which convicted. The latter measure was derived by counting the different dates on which sentences were passed to try to avoid the misleading effect of situations in which individuals received several convictions for what was essentially one act (for example, three separate convictions for taking and driving, driving without insurance, and driving without a licence). It was in fact very difficult to choose between these two, but the latter was marginally more clearly associated with unemployment length. In Table 3.28 a summary is provided of the number of occasions on which individuals in the samples had been convicted. Table 3.29 provides the same kind of information for the last 3 years.

Table 3.28. Number of occasions on which individuals were convicted (with percentages in brackets)

	Coventry	Hammersmith	Newcastle
None	297 (80)	187 (82)	266 (65)
One	30 (8)	14 (6)	38 (9)
2–4	28 (8)	12 (5)	45 (11)
5+	17 (5)	16 (7)	59 (14)

Table 3.29. Number of occasions in the last three years in which individuals were convicted (with percentages in brackets)

	Coventry	Hammersmith	Newcastle
None	331 (89)	205 (90)	353 (87)
One	25 (7)	17 (7)	26 (6)
More than one	16 (4)	7 (3)	29 (7)

Since numbers of convictions are difficult to generalize about in any case, being dependent upon both amounts of crime and police efficiency, it is difficult to comment on the way in which Newcastle differed from the other two areas. However, the fact that it differed but little as far as the last three years were concerned suggests that the presence in the Newcastle sample of men who have been on the margins of an insecure labour market for many years may have something to do with the larger numbers with old criminal records.

In no area was there a statistically significant association between number of convictions and unemployment length, but when only convictions in the last three years were considered a 'significant' association was found in Hammersmith ($p = <.02$). This, however, was an inverse relationship! Those with convictions appeared to get work more easily than those without. The important fact to take into account, and to explain this surprising finding, is that of course crime is a young man's 'trade'. In all three areas there was a strong ($p = <.01$) statistical association between crime in the last three years and age.

There are difficulties, however, in refining this analysis further, because the numbers with criminal records are rather small. Hence the numbers in individual age groups are even smaller. Table 3.28 provides some evidence of an association between whether individuals had been convicted in the last three years and unemployment length, but with low numbers the differences they indicate are not statistically significant.

In Table 3.30 the figures show that even with age taken into account there was still an inverse relationship in Hammersmith. However, it must be pointed out that the total numbers involved there were low amongst the two longer unemployment lengths (9 under 25s and 59 between 25 and 49). On the other hand both of the age groups considered above from Newcastle, and the under 25s in Coventry, show some tendency for longer unemployment to be associated with possession of a criminal record.

Table 3.30.   Numbers in various age groups in various unemployment lengths who had been convicted in the three years 1 October 1968 to 30 September 1971 (with percentages of age group and unemployment length group in brackets)

	Under 6 months	6 months to a year	Over 1 year
Coventry under 25s	7 (18)	11 (24)	23 (42)
Coventry 25–49	5 (9)	8 (13)	3 (9)
Hammersmith under 25s	8 (30)	1 (13)	0 (0)
Hammersmith 25–49	6 (13)	7 (13)	0 (0)
Newcastle under 25s	5 (15)	11 (29)	8 (28)
Newcastle 25–49	4 (10)	14 (17)	12 (16)

Some account was taken of types of crime. In Table 3.31 percentages are provided of men who had been convicted of various kinds of offences.

It will be clear from these figures that any attempt to analyse the unemployment experience of various types of criminals on the basis of these samples

Table 3.31. Numbers who had been convicted of various types of offences (with percentages in brackets)

	Coventry	Hammersmith	Newcastle
Offences against property	63 (17)	34 (15)	127 (31)
Fraud	12 (3)	6 (3)	25 (6)
Offences against persons (excluding sexual offences)	15 (3)	8 (4)	29 (7)
Sexual offences	10 (2)	5 (2)	9 (2)
Offences against National Insurance or Supplementary Benefits	1 ⁻ (0)	0 (0)	3 (1)

would be a fruitless exercise. The only category of any size, 'property offences', naturally correlates very well with numbers of convictions.

The great majority of the offences committed by the men in the three samples were remarkably petty. Not only are 'big-time' criminals pretty few and rather less likely to be found amongst the ranks of the registered unemployed, but it is also a reasonable supposition that those who were registered will have tended to be amongst the non-respondents.

The general lack of major criminals in the samples is further reflected in the information obtained on amounts of imprisonment. 8% of the samples in Coventry and Hammersmith and 12% in Newcastle had been in prison or borstal, but half of these had spent less than 5% of their lives since the age of ten 'inside'. The numbers who had been in prison during the period 1 October 1968 to 30 September 1971 were 2 in Coventry, 1 in Hammersmith and 0 in Newcastle.

There was some evidence, however, of an association between experience of imprisonment and unemployment length for the younger men in the sample. Those in the Coventry sample who had been in prison were statistically significantly ($p = < .05$) more likely to remain a longer time out of work.

Conclusions

At the end of the previous chapter brief social profiles of the samples were provided, showing that it was likely that a more thorough scrutiny of the data would produce evidence for the hypotheses about the importance of age, low skill and perhaps some of the measures of social inadequacy, at least as far as the samples from Coventry and Newcastle were concerned. Even at that stage Hammersmith's sample was identified as somewhat different, with a wider spread of skills and educational attainments amongst its members.

In this chapter the process of relating broad social characteristics to unemployment length has provided considerable evidence that many of the factors identified as important for the samples are indeed also correlates of long-term unemployment. The over-representation of the young in the samples was not reflected in any tendency for them to figure markedly amongst the long-term unemployed; on the contrary in all three areas a strong relationship was found between increasing age and increasing unemployment. Health was found to be related to prolonged unemployment, while mental health yielded some rather more ambiguous results, with Hammersmith standing out as a 'deviant' area. Some evidence was also found to suggest that the single are more prone to prolonged unemployment. These people were particularly in evidence in Hammersmith.

Hammersmith again figured as a rather different area when attention was paid to education and skill. In Newcastle and Coventry low qualifications and skills were shown to be strongly associated with unemployment length, while in Hammersmith this association was comparatively weak. In all three areas the evidence for an association between illiteracy and prolonged unemployment was rather inconclusive.

In Chapter 2 it was pointed out that many migrants from both inside and outside Britain were found in the Coventry and Hammersmith samples. Some rather confusing evidence was found on the relation between migration to the areas and unemployment length, with the mobile appearing to be slightly less prone to prolonged unemployment than the immobile; while the data on migrants from the 'Black Commonwealth' suggested that such people face greater employment problems in Hammersmith than in Coventry.

The information on the significance of criminal records did not yield the strong association expected between criminal record and long unemployment. Again difficulties seemed to arise because of the impact of more significant factors. It was suggested that the behaviour of men in this group, and possibly in other 'socially marginal' groups, tended to render the dependent variable, unemployment length, measured in terms of registration with the Department of Employment, rather unreliable.

Some of the difficulties of interpretation which have been suggested here led the authors to adopt a special multi-variate analysis technique to sort out some of the interactions between different variables. The reader will therefore find that many of the themes in this chapter are taken up again in Chapter 6, when the results from using that technique are reported.

4 The backgrounds and circumstances of the unemployed

Introduction

Considerable attention has been paid in Chapter 3 to factors which differentiate men with longer periods of unemployment from those with less, unemployment being measured in terms of the spell which they were experiencing at the time of the interview. Here current experience is placed in the context of past unemployment and job mobility and the possibility of a generative relationship between the two explored. In addition, the material circumstances and living conditions of the unemployed are described and investigation made of hypotheses which suggest that a high level of benefits relative to earning capacity acts as a disincentive to returning to work.

Past Experiences of Unemployment

Fifty per cent of the Coventry sample, 52% of the Hammersmith sample and 65% of the Newcastle sample had their first experience of unemployment before they were 25. The figures for numbers who first experienced unemployment in their youth perhaps make better sense when related to age at the time of interview. They are thus presented in Table 4.1 for everyone over 25.

The widespread early experience of unemployment by men in all the samples is quite striking. Newcastle's figures predictably reflect the fact that job prospects have not been good in that area for a long while. It is interesting, however, that such a large proportion of the Hammersmith sample experienced unemployment when they were young. This must be partly a reflection of the fact that there are a substantial number of migrants of all kinds in the sample.

In each area the non-manual and skilled workers were much less likely to have experienced unemployment before they were 25 than the unskilled workers. In particular middle-aged unskilled workers in Coventry and Newcastle were highly likely to have had their first experience of unemployment before they were 25.

38% in Coventry said they had never been unemployed before; by contrast only 28% in Hammersmith and 20% in Newcastle had never been out of work before. At the other extreme, 7% in Coventry, 16% in Hammersmith and 19% in Newcastle said they had been unemployed over ten times.

It is instructive to look at the incidence of unemployment in the past by age groups (see Tables 4.2 and 4.3).

Table 4.1   Percentages in each age group first experiencing unemployment
             when under 25

	Coventry	Hammersmith	Newcastle
Age group			
25–9	66	52	77
30–4	50	25	66
35–9	22	27	59
40–4	29	42	45
45–9	10	29	45
50–4	17	64	38
55–9	19	46	48
60+	25	34	32

Table 4.2.   Percentages in each age group who had never been unemployed
              before

	Under 25s	25–49s	Over 50s
Coventry	36	31	49
Hammersmith	20	30	28
Newcastle	32	13	20

Table 4.3.   Percentages in each age group who had been unemployed over
              10 times before

	Under 25s	25–49s	Over 50s
Coventry	2	13	6
Hammersmith	21	12	20
Newcastle	3	25	22

These figures again bring out the tendency of the men in the Hammersmith
sample to have had a much greater amount of previous unemployment than
those in the Coventry sample. The Coventry sample had many men in it who
were experiencing unemployment for the first time, or who had at least had
very little unemployment before. The Newcastle men inevitably had lived under
the continual threat of unemployment, but the Hammersmith men were drawn

from that minority in their area who are continually vulnerable to short spells of unemployment. Presumably if the Coventry unemployment rate fell back to the Hammersmith level a similar minority in a sample taken there would be more prominent.

It is also interesting to note the strikingly high proportion of under 25s in Hammersmith with over 10 spells of unemployment behind them. This suggests a degree of movement in and out of work which would not be possible in Newcastle, where such individuals might soon find it well nigh impossible to get back into work.

In the middle age group in Hammersmith there is a statistically significant association between numbers of times unemployed in the past and length of unemployment in the current spell ($p = < .01$). There is also a 'significant', though weaker ($p = < .05$), association of the same kind amongst the under 25s in Coventry. The other age groups in those two areas show a tendency towards a similar association, and so do all three age groups in Newcastle.

These findings accord well with evidence from other studies. Studies in the United States by Stein and Holland show that there a high proportion of the unemployed had previous unemployment and often recurrent unemployment. Sinfield draws the following conclusion from his international comparison of the evidence:

> The long-term unemployed had had greater experience of unemployment in the past and are likely to be more vulnerable to unemployment in the future as well. The longer unemployment has lasted, the less the chance of escaping from it. Yet few of the long-term unemployed, especially men, leave the labour force. (Sinfield, O.E.C.D., 1968, p. 16).

The contrast between Coventry and Hammersmith noted above comes out again when the reasons why the unemployed men's jobs ended are examined. Redundancy stands out as a more significant cause of unemployment in Coventry than in the other areas. The figures for all three areas are set out in Table 4.4.

When the reasons listed in Table 4.4 were related to unemployment length no marked differences appeared, except for a tendency for those who lost their jobs for health reasons to have longer spells of unemployment.

However, there were some noticeable differences between the answers given by individuals in different age groups. In all three areas the over 50s were much more likely to have been made redundant or to have lost their jobs for health reasons. The under 25s, on the other hand, nearly as often said they had left because the job was unsatisfactory, or had 'just left', or had been dismissed. Only 28% of the under 25s in Coventry had been made redundant, while a

72

Table 4.4.   Why the last jobs ended (with percentages in brackets)

	Coventry	Hammersmith	Newcastle
Redundancy, end of a term of engagement etc	169 (47)	87 (39)	144 (37)
Dismissed, where no other reason applies	49 (14)	29 (13)	63 (16)
Health reasons	37 (10)	28 (12)	59 (15)
Domestic reasons	15 (4)	4 (2)	15 (4)
Left to better self	5 (1)	3 (1)	5 (1)
Left because job unsatisfactory	44 (12)	24 (11)	42 (11)
Left for no specific reason	16 (4)	15 (7)	21 (5)
Left or dismissed as result of an offence against the law	7 (2)	4 (2)	7 (2)
Seasonal termination of job	4 (1)	9 (4)	11 (3)
Other reasons	13 (4)	22 (10)	25 (6)

further 28% said they had been dismissed and 21% said they left because the job was unsatisfactory. The three commonest replies to this question from the under 25s in Hammersmith were: (1) made redundant 21%, (2) left for no specific reason 21%, and (3) left because the job was unsatisfactory 18%. In Newcastle 27% said they were made redundant and 21% said they had been dismissed, while the replies 'left because job unsatisfactory' and just 'left' were each given by 12%.

Most of the other British studies of unemployed men are studies of redundant workers. The only study which provides data which can be compared with the figures given in Table 4.4 is Sinfield's study of unemployment in North Shields. In that study 'more than two out of three men said they had been paid off by their last employers and one out of four said they had left their last job'. (Sinfield, 1970, p. 223). The figures above for numbers saying they had left their last job are broadly similar to Sinfield's, but the other reasons are spread over a wider range of categories, with between a half and a third giving answers implying lack of available work.

However Sinfield's general observation on this topic is pertinent: 'The distinction between voluntary and involuntary termination of a job — so important in deciding eligibility to state benefits and public attitudes towards unemployment – was often a shadowy and arbitrary one'. It is not possible in a survey of this kind to produce very satisfactory distinctions between reasons for the ending of jobs. In controversial cases the accounts men give are complicated, and are in any case presented from their own perspectives.

Information was collected on incidence of unemployment during the three years prior to selection for the sample. The number of spells of unemployment experienced by the men in the sample during the three years 1 October 1968 to 30 September 1971 are given in Table 4.5.

Table 4.5.   Percentages with different numbers of spells of unemployment in 3 years 1 October 1968 to 30 September 1971 (including the spell man was in when interviewed)

	Coventry	Hammersmith	Newcastle
One	42	38	39
Two	25	22	20
Three	10	15	19
Four	10	8	9
Five or more	14	17	13

The differences between the areas on these figures are very slight. The association between number of spells of unemployment and length of unemployment in the spell studied is not at all clear. In Newcastle there was a statistically significant inverse relation between the two, largely because of the very long-term unemployed with only one spell of unemployment, lasting in many cases 3 years. In the other areas there was just an absence of association. In the same way there was an absence of clear associations between spells of unemployment and age, health or skill, the main factors associated with length of unemployment. The younger men in the sample tended to be more likely to have had a number of spells of unemployment; so too did the less skilled. The disabled were less likely to have had a number of spells of unemployment, except in Coventry where they had had more spells than the non-disabled.

In general it would seem to be that the use of a three year period for the tracing back of records is rather short for comments on the incidence of frequency of unemployment in poor economic conditions. In Newcastle no one who is seriously vulnerable to unemployment will experience a large number of spells of unemployment in a short period, because he will tend to get stuck out of work. In Hammersmith and Coventry the situation was more confusing because, while on the one hand there may have been a tendency for the young,

74

low skilled and unfit to experience a number of spells of unemployment, at the time of the survey the deteriorating employment situation blurred the picture.

Job Mobility

Although this period may be unrepresentative of total working life, it is possible to minimise distortion by analysis according to age group. In addition, the sample were asked to give the length of time they had worked in their longest jobs.

Hammersmith and Newcastle represented the extremes in the samples. Job mobility was greatest in the London area, where almost a fifth of the men interviewed had held five or more jobs over the three year period. It was the lowest in Newcastle, which differed from the other two areas in that a considerable proportion of the sample (18.5%) had been out of work throughout the entire period. Although the difference in employment opportunities between the South and the North is clearly shown in these contrasted statistics, it is interesting that in all three areas the majority of men (between 50—60%) had held 1—2 jobs and approximately 20—25% 3—4 jobs.

Table 4.6.   Number of jobs held over period 1 October 1968—1 October 1971

	Coventry %	Hammersmith %	Newcastle %
No job	5.9	6.2	18.5
1	37.7	32.0	30.7
2	21.1	19.6	19.2
3	11.0	12.9	12.7
4	10.4	10.2	6.3
5—9	12.7	16.0	11.7
10+	1.1	3.1	0.7
Total No.	355	225	410
%	(100)	(100)	(100)

Job mobility was closely associated with age in all three areas, although the pattern was rather different in Newcastle. Table 4.7 shows the relatively high number of job changes made by the 24 and under age groups in Coventry and Hammersmith (between three-tenths and a third had held five or more jobs over this period) and the increasing stability of the middle and older age groups. Even among the over 50s, however, between a fifth and a third of the samples had worked in 2–4 jobs and in Hammersmith almost a tenth had held five or more jobs. The levelling off of moves in employment is likely to be the outcome of a number of factors, but is probably related most closely to stages in the family life-cycle, a man being most mobile while he is single (and is also testing out different kinds of employment and assessing his earning capacity) and less so once he has dependents. Employment opportunities also no doubt decrease for certain skill levels as age increases and again short-term contract work in some occupations and industries will influence the number of job moves made. In Newcastle, as was noted earlier, the likelihood of having remained out of work throughout the whole 3 year period, and thus having had no jobs at all, increased markedly with age.

Table 4.7.   Job mobility and age. Numbers in each age group who had held different numbers of jobs over period 1 October 1968 to 30 September 1971 (with percentages in brackets)

| | Age group | | |
Numbers of jobs held	Under 25	25–49	Over 50
Coventry			
0	7 (8)	7 (5)	7 (6)
1	14 (16)	42 (29)	77 (63)
2–4	41 (47)	79 (54)	31 (26)
5+	26 (30)	19 (12)	5 (5)
Hammersmith			
0	4 (11)	3 (3)	7 (8)
1	2 (6)	33 (29)	43 (49)
2–4	18 (50)	48 (45)	30 (34)
5+	12 (33)	23 (23)	8 (9)
Newcastle			
0	8 (9)	23 (12)	45 (37)
1	26 (28)	54 (28)	46 (38)
2–4	45 (48)	86 (43)	26 (21)
5+	14 (15)	33 (17)	4 (3)

In Coventry and Hammersmith there was a close relationship between skill level and mobility and in Newcastle between skill level and total unemployment, over the three year period. The unskilled and semi-skilled were over-represented amongst the occupationally mobile in the Midlands and in London, while in Newcastle more proportionately of those entirely out of work were unskilled.

There was a similar association between birthplace and job mobility in Hammersmith and Coventry and between unemployment throughout the three year period and birthplace in Newcastle.

Coventry-born men were notably more mobile than those born elsewhere in the British Isles or overseas, but in Hammersmith men born in the Greater London area were rather more stable in their employment than migrants from overseas. There was a greater tendency in the North for Newcastle-born men to have remained out of work during the entire period.

Marital status was also related to the number of job moves made, although this will be for the most part a reflection of the significant relationship between age and mobility. In Coventry and Hammersmith more single men proportionately had changed their jobs frequently and rather more of the single remained out of work for the entire period.

Incomes

Table 4.8 sets out the amounts of money the men in the samples typically 'took home' from their last jobs.

Table 4.8 demonstrates that the Newcastle sample differed from the samples from the other two areas in the way expected from an inspection of average earnings figures for all workers in that city. It should be noted, however, that many more men in the Newcastle sample had been out of work a long while, so that the figures they quoted were often likely to be below the wage rates being paid for such jobs by October 1971. High inflation at that time would quickly have made old wage rates out of date. Within each area there were also differences between groups of unemployed men of a mostly predictable kind. In Coventry men whose last jobs were in skilled manual work had markedly higher incomes than those previously employed in either non-manual work or semi- or unskilled manual work. Only about 20% of the skilled earned less than £20 per week as against 45% of the non-manual workers, 47% of the semi-skilled and 51% of the unskilled. A similar pattern applied in Hammersmith, with 30% of the skilled earning under £20 as against 32% of the non-manual workers, 55% of the semi-skilled and 76% of the unskilled. In Newcastle, on the other hand, the differences were much less marked, with the four groups all having between 53% and 60% earning less than £20, with non-manual workers doing best and semi-skilled workers worst.

Table 4.8.   Amounts of 'take home' pay from last jobs (with percentages in brackets)

	Coventry	Hammersmith	Newcastle
Under £10	13 (4)	5 (3)	28 (7)
£10–14.99	44 (13)	38 (20)	79 (21)
£15–19.99	68 (20)	42 (22)	102 (27)
£20–24.99	75 (22)	34 (18)	68 (18)
£25–29.99	65 (19)	35 (18)	53 (14)
£30+	71 (21)	38 (20)	49 (13)

There were some interesting differences between amounts earned in last jobs according to the industrial sectors in which the men were employed. In Coventry only 25% of the men who were in manufacturing industry reported last earnings of under £20 per week, as against 55% in construction and 76% in services and public administration. The figures for those earning under £20 in the same three 'industrial' sectors in Hammersmith were 35%, 35% and 64%, and in Newcastle 49%, 46% and 64%. So in each area those who had been in service industries or public employment had had the poorest wages.

Some interesting figures emerged on the relationship between last pay and age, with the under 25s standing out as markedly the worst paid. This is an important fact to bear in mind in relation to the instability of this group as employees. In Coventry 67% of the under 25s had earned under £20 a week, as against 27% of the 25–49s and 27% of the over 50s. In Hammersmith a similarly high proportion, 69%, of the under 25s earned under £20, as against 33% and 54% in the other groups. In Newcastle the elderly and the young group appeared to have fared nearly equally badly, but here again it is important to remember that many of the elderly had not worked for some considerable time and that wage rates have changed markedly over the recent past. In Newcastle, the percentages in the three age groups who had earned under £20 were 69%, 42% and 66%. There were comparable differences in last earnings between the married and the single, which were presumably but reflections of the age differences.

There were also differences between the disabled and non-disabled (using the self assessment criteria) in amounts earned in last jobs. In Coventry 44% of the disabled and 35% of the non-disabled had earned under £20 per week. Comparable figures for Hammersmith were 61% and 41%, and for Newcastle 65% and 52%.

Despite these widespread low earnings, most of the men in the samples had been getting more in work than their total incomes while out of work. These figures are reported in Table 4.9. In computing these figures it was not necessary to depend solely upon information provided by the men. The figures for unemployment benefits and supplementary benefits were collected from official records.

Table 4.9.   Amounts of income in week ending 1 October 1971 (when almost all the sample were out of work) (with percentages in brackets)

	Coventry	Hammersmith	Newcastle
Under £10	170 (49)	89 (42)	158 (39)
£10–14.99	62 (18)	54 (25)	81 (20)
£15–19.99	63 (18)	34 (16)	98 (24)
£20–24.99	41 (12)	18 (8)	46 (11)
£25–29.99	9 (3)	9 (4)	16 (4)
£30+	4 (1)	10 (5)	4 (1)

It is instructive to compare amounts of take home pay in last jobs with income while unemployed. Both of these were tabulated in £5 bands for people with at least 4 weeks unemployment prior to their interview (the figures for people with shorter periods of unemployment would be unrepresentative as social security benefit amounts tend to be abnormal during this period). It was found that 5% in Coventry, 13% in Hammersmith and 12% in Newcastle had incomes when out of work in the £5 bracket above that in which their income in their last job fell. A further 9% in Coventry, 13% in Hammersmith and 25% in Newcastle had incomes in the same £5 bracket as their normal earnings.

There seems to be an association between length of time out of work and possession of an income above the level of last pay. This is shown in Table 4.10.

Before concluding anything about the possible impact of a high income as a deterrent to seeking work, it is necessary to observe that with inflation any pay rate from a year or more ago will tend to seem rather low, and that therefore the longer men were out of work the more likely that their past earnings would be below their current income levels. It was therefore considered whether a more appropriate comparison with income would have been with answers on the lowest rate of pay acceptable. A rather similar pattern emerges when this is done, though the numbers with acceptable pay levels above their income were rather fewer (6 in Coventry, 20 in Hammersmith and 29 in Newcastle)

79

and this seems likely to be a less reliable measure to use than last pay.

Table 4.10. Percentages of various unemployment lengths with incomes above last pay levels (men out of work under 4 weeks on 1 October 1971 excluded)

	Under 6 mths.	6 mths. to 1 year	Over 1 year
Coventry	2%	4%	7%
Hammersmith	7%	13%	21%
Newcastle	8%	12%	13%

There is one question that needs to be dealt with as far as any relation between income and other factors is concerned. This is whether many of the longer term unemployed who appear to have had higher incomes when out of work were in fact the recipients of income which would continue whether or not they were out of work. It was found that a substantial number of the unemployed with incomes above the level of their pay in their last job had other, 'non-benefit', income. This amounted to 7 of the 12 in Coventry, 19 of the 21 in Hammersmith, and 37 of the 41 in Newcastle. The income involved will normally have been family allowances, with a few receiving private pensions or with earning wives.

Finally, to infer from the figures quoted above that a high out of work income relative to typical pay is a deterrent to seeking work is to assume that the demand for labour has no impact in this situation. The men who were out of work a long while tended to be elderly, unskilled and in indifferent health; these were likely to have been the main determinants of both their low pay in the past and their long unemployment in the present. It was the last pay of the long-term unemployed that was low, not the high income that was the source of the relationship discussed above, as a comparison of Table 4.11 with Table 4.8 makes clear.

Earlier some brief references were made to income levels considered acceptable by the men in the sample. The question asked was 'Including overtime earnings what is the lowest level of weekly take home pay you would accept?' The main hypothesis to be tested was that men who would only accept high levels of pay would find it more difficult to get work. There was no evidence for this when a comparison was made between lowest acceptable pay and unemployment length. Such a crude comparison was bound to be unsatisfactory, since more highly skilled or qualified men are likely both to demand higher pay

80

levels and to be able to get work more easily. This was confirmed by a statistically significant association ($p = <.02$) between acceptable pay level and registered occupation in Coventry and Hammersmith. There was also a 'significant' association in all three areas between lowest acceptable pay and age, with the young and the elderly tending to be prepared to accept less than the middle age group. Presumably this was associated with a link between acceptable pay levels and domestic commitments.

Table 4.11.   Amounts of take home pay from last jobs — men out of work
                over a year only (with percentages in brackets)

	Coventry	Hammersmith	Newcastle
Under £10	3 (4)	2 (5)	15 (10)
£10–14.99	15 (18)	17 (40)	41 (26)
£15–19.99	22 (26)	8 (19)	46 (29)
£20–24.99	19 (22)	4 (10)	20 (13)
£25–29.99	14 (16)	6 (14)	20 (13)
£30+	12 (14)	5 (12)	14 (9)

Looking at the semi- and unskilled workers only, 40% in Coventry, 49% in Hammersmith and 55% in Newcastle were prepared to accept less than £20 per week. The comparable figures for men out of work over a year were 48% in Coventry, 64% in Hammersmith and 55% in Newcastle. The relation between acceptable pay levels and length of unemployment was only statistically significant in Coventry, and when age was taken into account, too, the only statistically significant differences in the semi- and unskilled worker group were amongst the over 50s in Coventry and the 25–49s in Hammersmith. There were no 'significant' differences amongst the non-manual and skilled workers.

Such evidence as there is certainly does not support the hypothesis that those who expect the most pay stay out of work longer; rather, it tends to point in the opposite direction. An alternative hypothesis is that workers who have been out of work a long while tend to lower their demands. This was best tested by relating acceptable pay levels to the length of unemployment that had already been experienced when the question was asked. Table 4.12 provides the evidence on this for semi- and unskilled workers in the middle age group (25–49) only.

Only in Coventry was an association between low levels of acceptable pay and long unemployment particularly clear. In Coventry alone there was a statistically significant association between low pay expectations and long

Table 4.12. Percentages prepared to accept less than £20 p.w., semi- and unskilled workers between 25 and 49 by length of unemployment before interview

	Under 3 months	3–6 months	6–9 months	9–12 months	Over 12 months
Coventry	14	20	28	29	60
Hammersmith	38	15	33	–	100
Newcastle	49	31	50	46	42

unemployment for semi- and unskilled workers, and, when age was also taken into account, for under 25s in those skill brackets.

An examination of the relationship between acceptable pay levels and unemployment lengths tends to indicate, to a slight degree, a similar conclusion to that reached when last pay and income when unemployed were compared, namely that the longer term unemployed were people who were normally, and expected to be, in low pay brackets.

Most men received 'earnings related supplements' to their unemployment benefit for the first six months of their unemployment. 110 of the Coventry sample (30%), 57 of the Hammersmith sample (25%) and 75 of the Newcastle sample (18%) were receiving this addition to their benefits at the time when the samples were selected. It is sometimes argued that the 'earnings related supplement' has the effect of deterring men from getting work again quickly, because it further reduces the hardship of unemployment. This is a difficult hypothesis to test, because the men who were still getting this addition had naturally not experienced very long unemployment by the time they were included in the samples. However, when unemployment lengths after the interview period were examined in order to try to test the above hypothesis, there was certainly an absence of evidence to support it. (See Table 4.13). In one area, Newcastle, there was a statistically significant tendency for those without earnings related supplement to remain unemployed the longest ($p = <.01$).

Unemployment benefit itself is paid to men who are unemployed for a period up to twelve months, if they have been paying contributions as employed workers for specific periods before they fall out of work. The actual qualification rules are rather complicated and it would be unnecessarily tedious to set them out here. Once he registers as unemployed, to qualify for unemployment benefit a man has to establish that he is unemployed and is capable of and available for work. In addition, if he is held to have refused work without good

Table 4.13. Percentages of those with various unemployment durations after 1 October 1971 who were receiving earnings related supplements to unemployment benefit on 1 October 1971

	Under 3 months	3–6 months	6 months or over
Coventry	32	32	28
Hammersmith	22	33	26
Newcastle	33	18	14

cause or to have been at fault in losing a job (because he left it without just cause or was sacked for misconduct for example), he may have his benefit stopped for up to six weeks.

There are no rules disqualifying a man from receiving unemployment benefit on the grounds that he has other income, so long as he is not being paid wages. By contrast the other source of state help for unemployed men is dependent upon calculations which relate their needs to their financial resources. This is supplementary benefit. The great majority of men who have exhausted their entitlement to unemployment benefit, or have lost it in some other way, inevitably have to apply for supplementary benefit. In addition, men who feel their unemployment benefit to be insufficient will also often apply for supplementary benefit.

Table 4.14 sets out the numbers getting various combinations of benefits.

In Newcastle all four men with no income at all had been out of work under three months, but in Coventry only four in this category had been out of work under three months and thirteen had been out over six months, while in Hammersmith nine had been out less than three months and six more than six months.

To throw further light upon the extent of poverty amongst the men in the samples the total incomes of householders were compared with their supplementary benefits entitlements. In order not to exaggerate the numbers with incomes below supplementary benefits levels a number of precautions were taken:

(a)   Only the incomes of men who were married and were householders were considered, since it was impossible to be sure that any assessments made of the domestic commitments of men not in these categories would correspond with those made by the Supplementary Benefits Commission.

(b)   Men who had been out of work less than four weeks were excluded from consideration on the grounds that their social security income would

Table 4.14.   Numbers out of work 4 weeks or more with various sources of
               income (percentages in brackets — reading across)

	Supplementary benefit and un-employment benefit	Supplementary benefit only	Unemploy-ment bene-fit only	No benefit but had other income	No Income at all
Coventry	42 (15)	86 (31)	127 (46)	5 (2)	18 (6)
Hammersmith	41 (22)	31 (17)	87 (48)	7 (4)	17 (9)
Newcastle	75 (21)	164 (46)	105 (30)	5 (1)	4 (1)

have been unlikely to have 'settled' down in such a short period. This safeguard
also had the effect of excluding the majority of the men with their unemployment benefits disallowed on account of the circumstances under which they
lost their last jobs.

   (c)   In addition all men who had been unable or unwilling to disclose any
part of their or their wives' incomes were excluded from consideration, together
with all those who had any earning members (other than wives) in their households.

   (d)   It was necessary when calculating the amounts of supplementary
benefits due to dependent children to assume that all children were under five,
and thus only entitled to the minimum of £1.70.

   (e)   Men with incomes less than £1 below their assessed 'supplementary
benefit levels' were not counted as falling below such levels. This precaution
was taken because it was impossible to be precise about everything that might
be taken into account in a supplementary benefits assessment, for example
extras included in rent commitments and savings.

   The findings on the extent of poverty, as defined in this very cautious and
stringent way, are set out in Table 4.15.

   There are small but not insignificant numbers falling clearly below 'supplementary benefit levels', and it is perhaps surprising that about half of them
were nevertheless in receipt of supplementary benefits. This is difficult to
explain. Some of them will have low incomes because they have 'wage stops',
to prevent their incomes exceeding their earnings capacities. In fact this is likely
to explain the situation in the cases of 11 men with 4 children or more. Otherwise it is difficult to analyse the circumstances of this small group much further.
Obviously, in a few cases the interviewers did not secure all the information
about these men available to the Supplementary Benefits Commission.

Table 4.15.   Married householders out of work over 4 weeks. Numbers with
              incomes above and below £1 less than supplementary benefit
              levels (with row percentages in brackets)

	Income	
	Above	Below
COVENTRY		
In receipt of supplementary benefits	51 (81)	12 (19)
Not in receipt of supplementary benefits	43 (83)	9 (17)
Totals	94 (82)	21 (18)
HAMMERSMITH		
In receipt of supplementary benefits	30 (86)	5 (14)
Not in receipt of supplementary benefits	37 (79)	10 (21)
Totals	67 (82)	15 (18)
NEWCASTLE		
In receipt of supplementary benefits	116 (83)	23 (17)
Not in receipt of supplementary benefits	48 (83)	10 (17)
Totals	164 (83)	33 (17)

Otherwise, it seems likely to have been the case that some of these men with
low incomes will have failed to secure adjustments to their social security
incomes to take account of changed circumstances. For example, on inspection
of the questionnaires it appeared possible that in a number of cases the termination of wives' earnings might have gone unreported.

It is recognised that there are considerable difficulties involved in judging
poverty levels by reference to the very complex supplementary benefit standards.
However, this particular exercise has been conducted with extreme care. From
it there seem to be grounds for concluding that a not insubstantial minority of
the unemployed receive exceptionally low weekly incomes on account of their

85

failure to apply for all help to which they are entitled, either because they do not apply for supplementary benefits or because they are slow to report changed circumstances when they are getting benefits.

As far as the whole sample is concerned, regardless of length of unemployment, and regardless of whether or not they were householders, it was found that 61% in Coventry, 70% in Hammersmith and 54% in Newcastle were getting unemployment benefits, with or without supplementary benefits. 41% in Coventry, 35% in Hammersmith and 64% in Newcastle were getting supplementary benefits.

Typically those without unemployment benefit who were getting supplementary benefit had exhausted their entitlement to unemployment benefit, or had deficient insurance contribution records. In Coventry 102 men were in this category and 82% of them were getting supplementary benefits. The corresponding figures for Hammersmith were 41 and 71%, and for Newcastle 181 and 97%. It is significant that in these figures the Newcastle sample is shown to contain markedly fewer people who did not seem to be claiming benefits to which they were entitled. It may perhaps be suggested that in the other two areas the past levels of prosperity and the present lower levels of unemployment provide more independent sources of money upon which unemployed men can draw; that people in those areas are less accustomed to seeking relief; and that in the area of continued high unemployment applicants for benefit are encouraged by a more sympathetic response on the part of officials.

Only a very small group in the sample, at the time the sample was selected, had their unemployment benefit suspended or disallowed for six weeks for losing jobs in circumstances in which they were deemed to be at fault. There were 26 in this category in Coventry, 13 in Hammersmith and 5 in Newcastle. From these groups there was a surprisingly low number getting supplementary benefits to replace the missing unemployment benefit; 12 in Coventry, 2 in Hammersmith and 2 in Newcastle.

A comparison was made between the answers given by men to questions about whether or not they were getting various types of benefits and what the true situation was. In Coventry 281 men said they were getting unemployment benefit. In fact 50 of those men had exhausted their right to unemployment benefit. In addition 10 had their benefits suspended or disallowed and 13 were not yet rated. It should be added, however, that the latter kinds of mistakes could well occur because the man was getting benefit when interviewed and mis-remembered the date his benefit started. This could not have been the case with the 50 whose benefit was exhausted. 89 men in the Coventry sample said they were not getting unemployment benefit; in fact 16 of these were getting it.

In Newcastle 265 said they were getting unemployment benefit when in fact only 199 of them were. 63 of those who were wrong had exhausted their benefits. 146 said they were not getting unemployment benefit; 23 of these were.

In Hammersmith 173 said they were getting unemployment benefit. Only 26 of them were wrong, 17 of them because they had exhausted their entitlements. 48 said they were not getting benefit; 8 of them were wrong.

Most of those who said they were getting unemployment benefit when they were not were in fact getting supplementary benefits. The fact that so many were wrong suggests that they were unable to distinguish between insurance benefits and supplementary benefits, an interesting indication of the low salience of the distinction between contributory and non-contributory benefits, a distinction which has been traditionally regarded as important.

A similar confusion existed over 'earnings related supplement' to unemployment benefit. In the three areas together 31% of those who said they were getting it were not in fact, and 11% of those who said they were not getting it were getting it.

The men were less confused as to whether or not they were getting supplementary benefit, though even here the numbers who got it wrong were quite considerable. In Coventry 26% who said they were getting supplementary benefit were not, and 19% who said they were not were in receipt of it. In Hammersmith the percentages getting it wrong were 28% and 6%. In Newcastle the percentages wrong were 13% and 20%.

There was only one other source of other income which was at all common, Family Allowances, received by 79 in Coventry, 40 in Hammersmith and 120 in Newcastle. 25 in Coventry, 21 in Hammersmith, and 18 in Newcastle said they had 'occupational' pensions. 34 in Coventry said their wives were earning. The numbers saying this in Hammersmith and Newcastle were 35 and 40 respectively. No other sources of income were in any way as significant as these three, so that in general it can be said that few of the unemployed were receiving payments from any sources other than the state.

Redundancy Pay

In Coventry 169 men said they were made redundant from their last job. 111 (29% of the whole sample) of these said they received redundancy pay and 93 of them were prepared to tell the interviewer how much they got. In Hammersmith 87 said they were redundant, 39 (17% of the sample) said they got redundancy pay and 35 reported the amount. In Newcastle the numbers in each category were 144, 44 and 39. In that area, then, only 8% of the sample said they had received redundancy pay.

The percentages with various amounts of redundancy pay are set out in Table 4.16.

The lower figures both of numbers getting redundancy pay and amounts of pay in Newcastle are a clear reflection of the persistence of poor employment prospects in that area. By contrast in Coventry there were a substantial number of men who had received quite large amounts of redundancy pay. Since redundancy pay is calculated by reference to pay at the time of redundancy multiplied by years of service, this is a reflection of the way in which a long period of stable prosperity in Coventry was broken during 1971.

The typical recipient of a large amount of redundancy pay was skilled and elderly. In fact there was a close association between age and whether redundancy pay was received, and an obvious relationship (because of the way it was calculated) between age and amount of redundancy pay. When age was taken into account no association between redundancy pay and unemployment length was apparent.

Table 4.16.   Percentages of those who received redundancy pay who got various amounts

	Coventry	Hammersmith	Newcastle
Up to £199	22	23	51
£200–399	20	29	13
£400–599	13	20	18
£600–799	16	9	8
£800+	30	20	10

The strong association between high redundancy pay and advanced age meant that the group taking home quite large sums were often out of work for very long periods. Therefore, while it might appear that some men are 'doing very well' out of redundancy, it is important to recognise that any gains tended to have been dissipated by long unemployment. Of the 34 men in Coventry who got over £800 redundancy pay, 12 were out of work over a year, and only 5 were out less than 6 months.

Housing

Information was collected on the housing circumstances of all the sample, but only the information collected on men who were themselves household 'heads' or who described their wives as 'heads' is presented in this section. This means that only men who were themselves owners or tenants, plus people in non-family boarding situations are included in the figures on housing that follow.

In Coventry this covered 67% of the sample and in Hammersmith and Newcastle 79% and 76% respectively. Of the rest the majority were living in the home (for the most part a house rather than a flat) of a parent or other relative and a very small number with a friend. Table 4.17 provides information on the kinds of accommodation occupied by household heads. The differences between the three areas are very much as would be expected, given housing conditions in each place.

Table 4.17. Kinds of accommodation occupied by household heads (with percentages in brackets)

	Coventry	Hammersmith	Newcastle
Whole houses	168 (72)	25 (14)	143 (48)
Purpose built flats or maisonettes	31 (13)	41 (23)	120 (40)
Converted flats	4 (2)	67 (38)	12 (4)
Rooms	9 (4)	39 (22)	19 (6)
Lodgers/Boarders	15 (7)	3 (2)	5 (1)
Others	6 (2)	1 (1)	1 (0)

Of those in houses, flats or rooms in Coventry, 44% were owners and 41% the tenants of the local authority, leaving only 15% renting privately (roughly half furnished, half unfurnished). In Hammersmith only 14% were owners and 24% local authority tenants, hence 29% rented privately unfurnished and 32% rented furnished accommodation. Owners were also few in Newcastle, 8%, but there 59% were local authority tenants. In Newcastle 20% were renting unfurnished, and 10% furnished. It would seem that particularly in Newcastle and Coventry local authority tenants were over-represented in the sample, although comparison (with 1966 sample census data on tenure patterns) can only be approximate. A higher proportion of the Hammersmith sample were renting private furnished accommodation than might have been expected.

Tenure patterns in each area were closely linked to the major variations in housing conditions. In Hammersmith, where private renting was the most common form of tenure and approximately 80% of men lived in flats or rooms, the standard of accommodation (measured in terms of size and amenity levels) was worst. The Coventry sample — split almost equally between owner occupation and local authority renting — enjoyed extremely favourable conditions, in comparison. These were the most spaciously housed (almost 70% of Coventry men lived in five or more rooms) and their accommodation had the highest standard of amenity (80% had sole use of all four amenities, see note to Table 4.18 for definition). In contrast, half of Hammersmith men lived in one to three rooms (30% in one or two rooms) and only 51% had sole use of the four basic amenities. Newcastle men were in an intermediate position, most commonly living in four or five rooms and with 69% possessing use of all four amenities.

Table 4.18 shows how clearly housing deprivation amongst the unemployed was linked with housing in the privately rented sector of the market, as it was quite substantial for tenants of private landlords but largely non-existent for owners and local authority tenants. It was in the private sector, too, where the smallest accommodation was to be found. (For instance, 84% of those living in one or two rooms in Hammersmith rented furnished accommodation from a private landlord).

Housing costs for the majority in Coventry and Hammersmith were within the range of £2.00 to £6.00, but half in Coventry and 40% in Hammersmith paid less than £4.00 per week. The amount paid for accommodation was predictably highest in Hammersmith (with a fifth paying £6.00 or more) and lowest in Newcastle, where 72% paid less than £4.00. Table 4.19 sets out the percentages of householders in each of the main tenure categories paying over £4.00 per week.

Despite the high proportion of local authority tenants paying over £4.00, the great majority paid less than £6.00. In Coventry 51% were paying between £4.00 and £5.99, in Hammersmith 57% and in Newcastle 36% were in this category. Furthermore, local authority tenants, as has been shown, were best provided for in terms of basic amenities, whereas the private rented sector, notably furnished accommodation, was most deficient. It would, therefore, seem that in this section of the market, especially in London, costs were high relative to the quality of accommodation occupied.

If the information on housing in this section is related to the information given in Chapter 2, based largely upon 1966 census data (which will over-estimate in some areas the proportions in bad housing or privately rented housing in 1971), there is little to suggest that the unemployed are worse housed than the rest of the population, although comparisons must be tentative. In fact, amenity deficiency in the housing of the unemployed tends to be rather less than in the population as a whole. The most likely reason for this is the significant over-representation of local authority tenants amongst the Newcastle and Coventry samples (and their slight over-representation in Hammersmith), the standard of accommodation in the public sector being notably above that in others. However, in Hammersmith, although the amenity levels of the unemployed are rather better than for the population as a whole, more live in furnished accommodation and rather more live in one or two rooms.

Table 4.18.   Amenity Scale[1]

	Owner Occupier	Local Authority Tenant	Private Unfurnished Tenant	Private Furnished Tenant	Total
Coventry					
Sole use of all four amenities	83%	93%	46%	27%	80%
Sole use of three	4%	6%	7%	–	5%
Sole use of two	5%	–	27%	20%	6%
Sole use of one	4%	1%	21%	20%	4%
Lacking all four amenities	3%	–	–	33%	4%
Hammersmith					
Sole use of all four amenities	79%	90%	43%	13%	51%
Sole use of three	13%	7%	6%	9%	8%
Sole use of two	8%	2%	22%	24%	16%
Sole use of one	–	–	27%	20%	14%
Lacking all four amenities	–	–	2%	33%	11%
Newcastle					
Sole use of all four amenities	86%	89%	29%	11%	69%
Sole use of three	5%	4%	26%	7%	9%
Sole use of two	–	3%	19%	21%	8%
Sole use of one	10%	3%	24%	11%	9%
Lacking all four amenities	–	1%	2%	50%	5%

(1)   The four basic amenities are:- fixed bath/shower, hot and cold water taps and an inside W.C.

Table 4.19. Percentages paying over £4.00 per week for housing, by tenure category

	Owner/ Occupiers	Local Authority Tenants	Renting Privately Unfurnished	Renting Privately Furnished	Total
Coventry	35	67	13	47	49
Hammersmith	39	78	45	60	57
Newcastle	15	38	7	25	27

This is not to deny that there are seriously disadvantaged groups amongst the unemployed; in all areas men with the lowest earning capacity (under £15 per week) were concentrated in the furnished sector, where amenity levels were lowest and accommodation most likely to consist of one or two rooms. In Hammersmith and Coventry there were disproportionate numbers of the unskilled dependent on this form of tenure, too, and it seemed that housing costs were higher relative to earnings than for the rest of the sample. (For example, in Coventry and Hammersmith, approximately 40% of the under £15 group were paying over 25% of their earnings for housing). Demographic information suggests that these households were largely the young (under 25), single and small households, but it also suggests that in Coventry and Hammersmith men of 50 and over living in private unfurnished accommodation were additionally at a disadvantage. This would accord with information from the National housing survey. (Woolf: *The Housing Survey in England and Wales,* para. 4.3).

Conclusions

In this chapter it has rarely been possible to relate the factors studied to unemployment length in the straightforward manner adopted in Chapter 3. The exception to this was provided in the early part of the chapter, where some interesting findings were reported on the past work and unemployment records of the men in the samples. In this section it was shown that the most unemployment prone elderly tended to have better past work records than the younger men in the sample, amongst whom the low skilled and poorly paid seemed particularly prone to insecure employment or job changing. This finding illustrates a particular problem with regard to the assessment of evidence on 'voluntary unemployment', since the men who appear most likely to abandon jobs needlessly are also those who get other work relatively easily.

On voluntary unemployment, a detailed examination was made of the hypothesis that men with high out of work incomes relative to their earning potential were likely to remain out of work longer. In fact, this hypothesis proved extraordinarily difficult to test, on account of the influence of other factors, which make for an association between poor employment prospects and low earning potential.

The other ingredient of the chapter was information on the incomes and housing conditions of the men in the sample, which threw some light on the extent of poverty amongst the unemployed, and on the low incomes of many such men even when they are in work. The findings on housing were quite encouraging, suggesting that very many of the unemployed (particularly outside London) are protected by the extensive local authority housing sector from suffering at the same time from both the deficiencies of the labour market and the deficiencies of the housing market.

5 Attitudes of the unemployed

Introduction

An analysis of the 'objective' factors determining the employment position of the men interviewed was made in the preceding chapters. In this chapter attention is focussed on the men's subjective experience of unemployment and some attempt is made to discover how motivations and expectations affect job prospects. It is generally recognised that individuals sharing a seeming parity of circumstances and opportunities may yet achieve varying degrees of success, the difference being accounted for by highly individual factors relating to the psychologies of the persons concerned. The following sections examine, therefore, the respondent's requirements of his job, how selective or flexible he would be in considering employment and the amount of effort he is prepared to expend on finding employment to his satisfaction.

Sources of Employment Problems

The men in the samples who were still unemployed at the time of their interview were asked whether any of a list of factors could be said to restrict their job prospects. To ensure comprehensive coverage of relevant factors up to three different answers were coded. There are six factors in all; the numbers mentioning each are set out in Table 5.1.

It is interesting how the problems that have already been identified as highly important disadvantages, age and health, were mentioned by large numbers, while the other factors were but little mentioned. 75 in Coventry, 42 in Hammersmith and 142 in Newcastle had criminal records, but only about a fifth of these people mentioned this as a disadvantage. It is interesting that the higher proportion mentioning 'psychological problems' in Hammersmith is matched by a higher proportion for whom there is independent evidence of mental illness. Finally, it is worth commenting on the low numbers mentioning domestic problems. Clearly it is right to treat this as an indication that for the men in these samples problems of this kind have a low significance as far as their job-seeking difficulties are concerned. However, it must be commented that issues of this kind are very difficult to investigate by straight-forward social survey interview techniques.

As far as sickness and age are concerned, men who said these factors were limiting tended to have long spells of unemployment. For example in Newcastle,

94

Table 5.1.   Factors said to be restricting prospects of getting work (percentages of total samples mentioning each in brackets)

	Coventry	Hammersmith	Newcastle
Physical health and disability	45 (12)	54 (23)	84 (20)
Recurrent illness	15 (4)	13 (6)	35 (8)
Domestic problems	15 (4)	11 (5)	22 (5)
Age	141 (40)	94 (41)	139 (34)
Psychological or emotional problems	9 (2)	21 (9)	20 (5)
Criminal record	17 (5)	15 (6)	26 (6)

while 20% of the total sample were out of work under six months, only 2% of those seeing disability as a limitation, 8% of those mentioning recurrent illness and 6% of those mentioning age were in the under six months category. Comparable figures for Coventry were 9%, 0% and 15% against 29% for the sample as a whole, and for Hammersmith 20%, 15% and 27% against an overall figure of 40%. On the other factors, respondents in Coventry and Newcastle describing themselves as having domestic, psychological or criminal record problems all suffered more unemployment than average. In Hammersmith, however, where 40% of the total sample fell in the under six months group, 27% of those with domestic problems, 53% of those with problems stemming from criminal records, and 57% of those with psychological problems had similarly short spells of unemployment. Presumably jobs of some kind were sufficiently easy to get in Hammersmith that the problems identified were of little actual relevance in determining employment prospects. It is not known, of course, how many of these men got satisfactory jobs or how many got jobs they were able to stay in. The figure for the psychological problem group is particularly striking as it correlates with similarly surprising findings with the Personal Disturbance scale. It is also necessary to bear in mind the qualification made in Chapter 3 about individuals ceasing to register as unemployed but not going back to work.

In Coventry 42% of the sample said that they considered that they had had difficulties in obtaining jobs in recent years and 16% said they had had difficulties in holding down jobs. The corresponding figures for Hammersmith were 48% and 21%, and for Newcastle 57% and 17%. In all three areas a greater proportion of the long-term than the short term unemployed answered these questions in the affirmative. The main reasons are given in Table 5.2. Up to two reasons were coded.

Apart from economic factors, age and health again appear to be recognised as the main sources of difficulties. In Coventry and Newcastle there were large numbers complaining about a lack of jobs at their 'skill level'. This may be linked with the finding in Chapter 3 on numbers who were not registered for skilled occupations although their last jobs were skilled.

Table 5.2.   Numbers mentioning various different sources of employment difficulties

	Coventry	Hammersmith	Newcastle
Health/Disability	28	30	53
Economic factors	24	16	44
Seasonal factors	9	1	13
Lack of jobs with sufficient pay	46	12	30
Lack of jobs at skill level	47	8	38
Domestic problems	7	2	8
Age	32	30	59
Bad work record	10	4	3
Criminal record	10	7	13
Racial discrimination	5	9	4
Others	21	49	45

Flexibility

A number of questions were asked about willingness to move, willingness to work away from home, readiness to accept training and distances men were prepared to travel to work.

87% of the Coventry sample, 88% of the Hammersmith sample and 81% of the Newcastle sample were not prepared to spend more than an hour getting to work. Each group was divided fairly evenly between those not prepared to spend more than half an hour travelling and those prepared to spend up to an hour. There was no noticeable difference between the respondents from the different areas, and no difference between men of different unemployment lengths in response to this question.

A question was also asked about the amounts men were prepared to spend on travel to work. The answers to this question were expressed as percentages of expected earnings. The range of answers on this was rather more marked than the range of replies to the question on travelling time. About 80% of the Coventry sample were prepared to spend 4% or more. In Hammersmith about 75% were prepared to spend this much and in Newcastle 70% were in these categories. Again no associations between the answers to this question and unemployment length were apparent.

The replies given to the two questions on travel to work were related to occupation. No marked differences were found between the occupational groups in any area in the time they were prepared to spend travelling to work or in the proportions of their income they were willing to spend on travel.

In each area the young appeared ready to spend more on travel and to spend more time travelling to work. In Coventry 85% of the under 25s were prepared to spend 4% of their income or more, as against 76% of the 25–49s and 74% of the over 50s. Corresponding percentages for Hammersmith were 82%, 72% and 62%; and for Newcastle the percentages were 74%, 65% and 62%. The evidence on travel to work time was not quite as clear cut as this, but pointed in the same direction.

In each area roughly the same proportions, just under 40%, expressed a willingness to work away from home. Most of the men who said this were quite prepared to conceive of this as involving extensive absence from home, for periods of between six months and a year. The men who said they would be prepared to work away from home tended, in each area, to be out of work for shorter periods. This difference was statistically significant in Hammersmith ($p = < .02$) and Newcastle ($p = < .01$). The great majority of those not wishing to work away from home cited 'domestic reasons' for not doing so.

There was little difference between the skill groups in willingness to work away, but not surprisingly the unmarried were much more willing to work away than the married. However, in all three areas those within the 'not married' (single and 'other' marital statuses) who were prepared to work away were statistically significantly more likely to have short spells of unemployment, and in Newcastle a similarly 'significant' distinction existed between the married who would work away and those who would not. This question was one of the few attitude questions which distinguished the long-term and short-term unemployed fairly clearly. However it was to some degree related to age. The rather weaker association when age is taken into account is shown in Table 5.3 and Table 5.4.

In each area a little over half the men expressed a willingness to move home in order to get work. There was a marked association between willingness to move and length of unemployment, though it was statistically significant ($p = < .01$) only in Hammersmith. When the sample was broken up into three age groups this association largely disappeared, except in Hammersmith where it remained significant for all three groups.

Table 5.3. Percentages prepared to work away from home by unemployment length (married men between 25 and 49 only)

	Under 6 months	6 months to 1 year	Over 1 year
Coventry	27	37	30
Hammersmith	32	24	0*
Newcastle	48	44	33

*Note: There was only 1 man in this category

Table 5.4. Percentages prepared to work away from home by unemployment length (unmarried men between 25 and 49 only)

	Under 6 months	6 months to 1 year	Over 1 year
Coventry	83	50	40
Hammersmith	68	63	20
Newcastle	80	64	30

Those unwilling to move gave a variety of reasons for this. They are set out in Table 5.5.

Table 5.5. Reasons for unwillingness to move (with percentages of all those answering the question on whether or not they would move).

	Coventry	Hammersmith	Newcastle
Age	50 (14)	22 (10)	33 (9)
Housing problems	27 (8)	10 (4)	22 (6)
Children's schooling	17 (5)	6 (3)	13 (3)
Friends and relatives	50 (14)	27 (12)	47 (12)
Other reasons	15 (4)	37 (17)	50 (13)

The numbers citing age as a reason for not moving are unsurprising; so is the strong association between this reply and unemployment length. On the other hand it is rather surprising that so few mentioned housing problems, while considerable numbers mentioned the fact they had friends or relatives in the area. The association between this reply and unemployment length is not particularly marked, yet it provides another indication that objective factors like age tend to be of much more marked importance than subjective factors of this kind.

It was suspected that the reply 'friends and relatives' above might be masking some other factor, or might be associated with particular occupation and age groups. But no clear differences were found between the age or occupation groups here, nor was it associated with disability or mental illness in any recognisable way.

A number of other studies of groups of unemployed men in Britain have attempted to investigate willingness to move or work away from home. 26% of Wedderburn's sample of redundant manual workers expressed a willingness to move to get work, and 30% of Kahn's redundant Birmingham car workers said they had considered moving, as did 37% of unemployed men on Tyneside interviewed by Richardson and West. Two studies, a national one on labour mobility quoted by Gittus and Gittus' own study on Merseyside, put their questions the other way round and found that 45% and 39% respectively required work near home. In the present study, as stated above, about half were prepared to move. Not surprisingly this is a higher proportion than those found in the redundancy studies, since many of the redundant men were not interviewed until after they got new jobs and nearly all of them had fairly good prospects of getting more work locally. The findings only diverge noticeably, therefore, from the 37% found by Richardson and West. Incidently, too, Richardson and West quoted housing as the major obstacle to removal (69 out of 96) while 33 listed ties to the area and 13 obligations to older relatives. It was surprising, therefore, that housing was mentioned so little by respondents from Newcastle or the other areas.

Government Training

The men interviewed were asked a linked series of questions about government training. A substantial number—44% in Coventry, 28% in Hammersmith, and 24% in Newcastle had no knowledge of government training at all. Only a very small proportion of the remainder had ever applied for training and only 6% in Coventry and Newcastle and 5% in Hammersmith claimed to have completed a course at some time in their lives.

A considerable number of those who claimed no knowledge of government training were comparatively recently unemployed. Eighty-one of the 163 in Coventry who said they had no information about government training had, at the time of the interview, been out of work under 3 months. Comparable figures for Hammersmith were 35 out of 65, and for Newcastle 40 out of 99. However, this leaves a substantial residue in each area who had been out of work long enough for it to be expected they might have heard about government training.

In Table 5.6 the percentages of each skill group who had no information about government training are set out for each area.

Table 5.6. Percentages of each skill group who had no information about government training

	Non-manual workers	Skilled manual workers	Semi-skilled workers	Unskilled workers
Coventry	48	42	36	53
Hammersmith	35	19	31	26
Newcastle	22	24	24	24

No very clear picture emerges from these figures, though the lack of knowledge on the part of the unskilled workers in Coventry is worth noting.

In each area half or more of those who said they had been rejected for training by the Employment Exchanges were unskilled. In Coventry 8 of the 12 so rejected were unskilled, in Hammersmith only 2 out of the 4 were in this category, but in Newcastle 35 men said they had been rejected and 26 of them were unskilled.

The men who said they knew about government training but had not applied were asked, 'Why not?' In each area over half of those asked this question replied they were not interested or felt no need for training or had trades already. It was certainly the case in both Coventry and Hammersmith that those giving replies of this kind were rarely long-term unemployed and were predominantly skilled.

In all three areas together 99 said they were ruled out for government train-'ing because of age. Of these, presumably only one, a man in his twenties, meant he thought he was too young. 88% of all those giving this answer were over 50.

There were few other answers given to the question about reasons for not applying for government training. Only 11 people said they thought the courses were no good, and only 17 said there was too long to wait for courses. 12 felt they were inadequately educated or qualified to benefit from courses, and 26 gave reasons connected with their unwillingness to live on a training allowance or stay away from home.

These findings on knowledge of government training can be related to Wedderburn's findings with a sample of redundant manual workers. 27% of the workers in her sample, who were still out of work when she interviewed them, did not know about government training; that is a comparable proportion to the Hammersmith and Newcastle samples, but a smaller percentage than in the perhaps rather more comparable Coventry sample. The majority of Wedderburn's sample who knew about government training did not consider applying.

Reference Groups

In the course of planning the research considerable thought was given to the possibility of identifying 'reference groups' for unemployed men, to test the hypothesis that men who remain out of work a long while are likely to have relatives and friends out of work too. The problem with this topic is that it is difficult to achieve any realistic and reliable means of identifying 'friends'. In the pilot survey men were asked whether they knew other people who were out of work. Many said they did, but when they were asked when and where they saw such people most of them gave the not very surprising reply 'when I sign at the Exployment Exchange'. There was little evidence of a more distinct pattern of association than that, and accordingly it was decided not to ask any questions about friends or acquaintances in the main survey.

However, some attempt was made to identify whether the unemployed men had fathers or brothers who were unemployed. In order to establish that such individuals were 'significant others' for the unemployed men they were asked if they saw their fathers or brothers once a month, or more often, and if they were of working age.

Only 14 in Coventry, 1 in Hammersmith and 26 in Newcastle had unemployed fathers whom they saw once a month or more often. Clearly, then, little could be deduced from this small sample. On the other hand there were a rather greater number with unemployed brothers, 32 in Coventry, 13 in Hammersmith and 40 in Newcastle. Furthermore there appeared, at first sight, to be some association between having an unemployed brother and lengthy unemployment. However, this was not found to be a statistically significant association, and in any case it can be hypothesised that such an association might be related to the possession of similar skill and education levels. This would appear to be the case, for when only the semi- and unskilled groups were examined there was really no evidence at all of an association between having unemployed brothers and unemployment length.

Job Satisfaction

A question was asked about the qualities men expected jobs to possess. They were presented with the list set out in Table 5.12, and were also invited to add other important things which they considered to be missing from the list. They were asked to state which three qualities, in order of preference, they considered 'the most important qualities for a job to possess'. Their first preferences are set out in Table 5.7 and all three preferences are given in Table 5.8.

Table 5.7. Important job qualities (first preferences) (with percentages in brackets)

	Coventry	Hammersmith	Newcastle
Interesting and satisfying work	170 (47)	107 (47)	122 (30)
Good pay	107 (29)	70 (31)	172 (42)
A good foreman/boss	24 (7)	13 (6)	17 (4)
Good working conditions	37 (10)	20 (9)	60 (15)
Satisfactory work-mates	11 (3)	14 (6)	17 (4)
Adequate off-work facilities	0 (0)	2 (1)	3 (1)
Others	3 (1)	0 (0)	2 (0)
Nothing is important	2 (1)	0 (0)	1 (0)
Don't know/Can't say	9 (2)	2 (1)	11 (3)

Three things, interesting work, pay and working conditions, dominate these preferences, but there are some interesting variations between areas. Pay appears most frequently in the lists of three preferences, but only in Newcastle does it head 'interest' on first preferences. It is interesting that both pay and working conditions are stressed more in the only 'traditional' working-class area of the three, while clearly 'instrumental' workers are less evident in Hammersmith and Coventry. This suggests that the less stressful economic conditions in the Midlands and the London area enable unemployed workers to place more emphasis upon work satisfaction.

There is some, but not a marked, association between seeking job satisfaction and skill level. In Coventry 52% of the skilled manual workers put 'interesting and satisfying work' as their first preference, as against 39% of the unskilled workers. In Hammersmith the comparable percentages were 47% and 28%, and in Newcastle they were 34% and 24%. In Coventry 25% of the skilled workers and 51% of the unskilled put pay first. In Hammersmith 15% of the skilled and 35% of the unskilled did this, while in Newcastle the percentages were very similar, 46% and 44%.

Table 5.8.   Important job qualities (all 3 preferences) (with percentages of total sample in brackets)

	Coventry	Hammersmith	Newcastle
Interesting and satisfying work	276 (74)	159 (69)	252 (62)
Good pay	290 (77)	191 (82)	358 (86)
A good foreman/boss	138 (37)	77 (33)	156 (38)
Good working conditions	188 (50)	123 (53)	227 (55)
Satisfactory workmates	92 (25)	71 (31)	164 (40)
Adequate off-work facilities	18 (5)	14 (6)	22 (5)

Respondents were next asked 'To what extent do you anticipate that you will be able to satisfy these requirements in the kind of job you usually do?' In all three areas a very high proportion (91% in Coventry, 83% in Hammersmith and 79% in Newcastle) said they expected either 'full' or 'some' satisfaction of their requirements. Their answers were divided roughly equally between the two replies.

It is instructive therefore to look more closely at the minority who said they expected to be unlikely to satisfy, or were sure not to satisfy, their requirements. Taking first the group as a whole, there was no pattern of association between these replies and unemployment length. There was not a very marked tendency for them to have low skilled occupations. In Hammersmith 25% of the unskilled gave replies of this kind, as did 24% in Newcastle, but in Coventry only 8% of the unskilled expected little work satisfaction. In fact such replies were nearly as common from the non-manual workers (12% in Coventry, 15% in Hammersmith and 25% in Newcastle) and it was the skilled who seemed most unlikely to expect to find their job unsatisfactory (7% in

Coventry, 11% in Hammersmith and 14% in Newcastle). Within the skill groups there was no pattern of association between expectation of finding a satisfactory job and unemployment length.

The replies to the question about anticipation of job requirement satisfaction were further analysed in relation to (a) the main kinds of requirements, good pay and interesting work, and (b) unemployment length.

Of those mentioning good pay amongst their requirements, 93% in Coventry, 82% in Hammersmith and 79% in Newcastle said they expected either 'full' or 'some' satisfaction of their requirements. In the three areas, 98%, 74% and 71% of those unemployed over a year gave similar answers. Therefore the long-term unemployed did not differ markedly from others in their expectation of being able to secure what they considered reasonable pay.

Of those mentioning interesting work amongst their requirements, 91% in Coventry, 84% in Hammersmith and 80% in Newcastle said they expected either 'full' or 'some' satisfaction of their requirements. The figures for those unemployed over a year were 95%, 76% and 79%.

There is little evidence therefore of marked differences between the expectations of various groups in the samples.

Job Hunting

The questions concerning the number of methods used to look for work during the current spell of unemployment and the relative success of these methods in securing an interview attempted to examine a number of points of interest. First was the question whether the number of techniques used was indicative of a willingness to look for work. It could be hypothesised that those with longer periods of unemployment in the current spell might be less willing to look for work than those with shorter periods of unemployment. Those with longer periods of unemployment might give up looking as a result of a realistic assessment of their job prospects, or it might be that the least diligent job hunters were out of work as a consequence of their lack of diligence.

Second was the question whether some methods of seeking work were consistently more likely to obtain an interview than others. This might be termed the 'effectiveness' measure.

Third, was the success of any job searching method largely attributable to the persons using the technique rather than the technique being generally more successful than any other?

The first point was examined by looking at the mean score of job searching methods used by length of unemployment in the current spell. The results are set out in Table 5.9.

There is little evidence here to suggest that the average number of techniques
104

used diminishes as unemployment in the current spell increases and hence little to suggest that men unemployed for a long period of time were less diligent in looking for work or less hopeful of finding work.

The four job seeking methods used most often were:

(i) enquiring at the Employment Exchanges, used by over 85% in all areas;

(ii) looking in local newspapers, something that around 80% did in Coventry and Newcastle and only about 10% fewer in Hammersmith;

(iii) calling at firms, a technique used by around 70% in all areas;

(iv) contacting former workmates, an approach claimed by over 50% in all areas.

Table 5.9.   Mean scores of job seeking methods used

| Area | Unemployment length | | | |
	0–12	13–25	26–38	39–51
Coventry	5.4	5.4	5.5	5.5
Hammersmith	4.8	5.5	4.9	5.2
Newcastle	4.6	5.3	4.8	4.2

| Area | Unemployment length | | | |
	55–77	78–103	104–55	156–82
Coventry	5.6	5.2	4.6	5.0
Hammersmith	5.1	6.3	3.3	2.0
Newcastle	4.5	3.7	3.8	4.2

Forty to fifty per cent in each area said that they had tried asking friends and relatives and writing to firms and around a third said they had tried telephoning firms. In Coventry a third had tried to get jobs through trade unions. The unions are an important source of access to jobs there; they did not appear to be at all important in this respect in the other two areas. Two-thirds of the Hammersmith sample said they had looked in national papers; these, of course, carry many London vacancies, so few from the other areas said they had consulted them. Other job seeking methods the men were asked about, which were however not widely used, were writing, private employment agencies, looking at trade papers and seeking help through welfare agencies. Apart from the exceptions mentioned, the job seeking techniques used were remarkably similar in the three areas.

In addition to looking at those techniques most frequently used, it was also possible to examine whether the most frequently used techniques were most effective in obtaining an interview. To do this an effectiveness index was constructed.

This index was calculated by dividing the total number of persons using the technique into the total number of persons securing an interview using the technique. A technique which was 100% successful scored 1.0, the least successful 0.0, and one where half the users obtained an interview scored 0.50. The four most effective techniques are listed and ranked in Table 5.10. These rankings can be compared with the rankings obtained for the proportions of job seekers using the various techniques.

Table 5.10.   Rank ordering of effectiveness index

Coventry		Hammersmith		Newcastle	
1. Employment Exchange	0.30	Writing to firms	.45	Employment Exchange	.35
2. Writing to firms	.28	Employment Exchange	.44	Calling at firms	.23
3. Calling at firms	.27	Calling at firms	.28	Private Agencies	.22*
4. Welfare, etc.	.20*	National Paper	.22	Writing to firms	.21

*Note: Few in the sample used these techniques and therefore these scores cannot be considered of significance

On the whole, none of the methods scored more than 0.45 (less than 50% effective) and the most effective technique was the Employment Exchange. The Employment Exchange was most effective in Coventry and Newcastle, although it ranked second after writing to firms in Hammersmith.

The scores on the effectiveness index, when compared with the proportions using a technique, show that the techniques used most often were also the most effective. The exception was the use of local newspapers, which ranked high as a method but low as an effective method. In part this was probably due to the fact that access to local newspapers was quite high, and men would only have to have glanced at the pages for this to qualify as using the method. Very little commitment to the technique was required. The use of a local newspaper was likely to be a method used indiscriminately by all those looking for work

106

and thus a large number of people whose chances of finding work through this method were low in fact still used the method. There was an absence of the self selection process which accompanies other job searching methods, such as 'writing', where there was probably a high degree of association between propensity to use the technique to secure an interview and the possession of skills necessary to obtain employment.

It is necessary to try to discover the extent to which a technique was success-ful because the people using it tended to be good employment prospects, and the extent to which a tecnique was effective in securing an interview regardless of the people tending to use it.

One would tend to think that techniques such as writing for jobs or con-tacting firms directly would be more effective when used by those groups with better job prospects, i.e. those with less unemployment, higher social class and in the 25–49 age group. This would be evidenced in the effectiveness index by holding the technique constant and looking for variations in the effective-ness score.

Effectiveness of technique did not in fact vary significantly in relation to age, class or length of unemployment for the techniques used by any consider-able number of men.

Attitudes to the Employment Exchange

A survey of unemployed men provided an opportunity to obtain an indication of the attitudes unemployed men have toward the Employment Exchange. Three questions were asked:

(a)   Do you think the Exchange have considered all the facts in your case?

(b)   Do you think the Exchange could have done more to help you find a job?

(c)   What are the most important ways in which the Exchange could have given you more help?

These questions formed only a small section of the questionnaire and are to some extent superficial. Furthermore, they were worded in such a way that they tended to encourage the expression of dissatisfaction. However, this should not be seen as an argument for ignoring the attitudes expressed completely. Firstly, these questions were an attempt to gauge consumer reaction from a group of people with whom the Exchange is most frequently in contact. Secondly, they provide an alternative view of the Exchange and its function from that obtained by essentially employer oriented questions. Thirdly, and this is of particular relevance to point (a) above, the Department of Employ-ment has expressed a concern that the Employment service should encourage

107

the individual to develop his potential, provide access to vocational guidance, occupational information and particulars of unfilled vacancies and provide help for the socially disadvantaged and longer term unemployed. These objectives rest on the assumption that the Exchange staff make every effort to sensitise themselves to the individual needs and problems of the clientele.

In answer to the question, 'Do you think the people at the Employment Exchange have considered all the facts in your case?', one third of those in the sample in each area who were looking for work said 'No' (Coventry 34%, Hammersmith 37% and Newcastle 32%). When asked the reason for claiming that all the facts in their case had not been considered, few respondents could provide a concrete answer. However, 18% in Coventry, 32% in Hammersmith and 17% in Newcastle gave answers that fell into one of the following categories:

(i)   failure to take account of previous job experience
(ii)   failure to take account of job preferences
(iii) failure to take account of family problems.

In response to the question, 'Could the Exchange have done more?', 35% in Coventry, 33% in Hammersmith and 40% in Newcastle said 'Yes'. The bulk of these claimed that the Exchange could have provided more job submissions or have shown more interest in some unspecified way.

There is evidence that a substantial minority felt some sense of dissatisfaction with the Exchange, but this was not articulated in any specific form except in a few cases. The request for more job submissions is open to a number of interpretations:

(a)   a belief that there were jobs but that men were not being submitted by the Exchange for some unknown reason, or
(b)   the feeling that job submissions were inadequate may have provided a concrete tag on which to hang other less easily expressed dissatisfactions.

Allowing for the fact that the cause of dissatisfaction with the Employment Exchange is a matter for further investigation, and accepting that the client may direct many of his frustrations at being unemployed towards the Employment Exchange, since it represents a point of regular contact with 'the system', the problem remains that one third of those using the Employment Exchange were dissatisfied with the treatment they received. Any attempt to improve the Employment Exchange as a service for the unemployed as well as the employer needs to take this into consideration.

Conclusions

There are considerable difficulties in including a very searching investigation of attitudes in a large-scale survey in which a questionnaire technique is used to elicit wide ranging kinds of information. The present study was supplemented

108

by a more detailed investigation of the attitudes of a sub-sample of young long-term unemployed men in Coventry; the results of this study will be reported in a later book, in which it is expected that it will be possible to go rather more deeply into some of the issues raised in this chapter. However, some interesting findings were reported here.

It was interesting to discover that men's subjective assessments of their employment problems tended to relate so well to the more objective findings. It was also interesting to discover that beneath the objective factors what must be regarded as motivational factors as much as direct predictions of intentions, such as willingness to move and work away from home, were associated with unemployment length. At the same time the findings on job searching techniques, which might have provided a more direct indicator of commitment to getting work, were not so revealing. It was also hypothesised that those expecting high job satisfaction might be expected to get work most readily, but this, too, was not found to be the case. On this line of investigation the considerable number looking for and expecting to get what they regarded as satisfying and/or well paid work was quite surprising.

Finally, questions on the Employment Exchanges and on training indicated considerable scope for the further development of these services for the unemployed, though here the shortage of comparable studies makes the possibilities for saying anything significant about these subjects severely limited.

6   The main findings: a further examination

There are several limitations to the techniques of analysis that have been used so far, i.e., plotting the distribution for variables against various categories of unemployment length and backing up the findings by means of chi squared tests of significance. The main limitations are as follows:

(a)   Where a number of variables are all shown to be significant it is impossible to provide any indication of their order of importance.

(b)   Where, as is very much the case with the present study, there are a large number of complex interactions between the variables it is difficult to disentangle all the possible relationships.

(c)   The process of controlling variables to detect specific interactions is made difficult by the fact that, despite the fact that the sample sizes used in the present study were quite large by British social survey standards, it is very difficult to avoid ending up with tables with small numbers in them from which little can be deduced. Accordingly there is a tendency for the impact of the less significant variables to be masked by the major ones which have to be controlled in analysis.

(d)   Where, as in this case, it is particularly interesting to compare different areas it is difficult by means of the description of a large number of separate cross tabulations to convey very clearly the major contrasts.

In order to try to overcome some of these difficulties the multi-variate analysis technique described in the next section was adopted.

The A.I.D. Programme

The Automatic Interaction Detector programme produced by Sonquist and Morgan was specifically designed for analysing survey material of the type collected for this study, and dealing with the type of problems that it encountered. In brief, the operation of the programme is designed to ascertain what is required in order 'to reduce the predictive error by a maximum amount'. (J.N. Sonquist and James N. Morgan, p. iv).

To put it simply, what occurs in the A.I.D. programme is that the computer scans a series of variables or predictors, which are fed into the programme, and chooses the one which contains within its coding categories a division or split that will reduce the predictive error (that is the sum of squares around the mean) by the greatest amount. That is, the programme selects variables responsible for explaining differences in unemployment length in order of importance. It repeats this process with the groups created by the previous split until the analysis is exhausted, either by not having sufficient numbers left, or because no predictor is capable of making a statistically significant difference, or because there is insufficient variance in the groups to warrant a split.

The output from this process states what splits have been made with which variables and which codes, giving the size of the mean for the group, together with the reduction of the variance and the total sum of squares. From this information the user can construct a diagram, which looks very much like a family tree, showing how the variables are related, and giving their order of importance. These diagrams are referred to as run maps. The analysis given below contains descriptions and comments on the run maps obtained using the survey data. The groups sorted out by the programme are described as 'advantaged' or 'disadvantaged' according to whether they have mean unemployment lengths $(\bar{X})$ lesser or greater than the overall groups from which they were derived.

The programme has some built in tests of statistical significance which prevent completely arbitrary or accidental splits, i.e. relationships that can appear due to sampling error, and also a limit on the minimum size of a group, beyond which it would be pointless to proceed. In this case the limit was set at the point at which new splits would otherwise create groups of 10 or less.

The aim of the programme is to generate hypotheses rather than to test them. It was never intended that the results of the A.I.D. analysis should be used without the backing of more conventional and conservative statistical analysis. What was hoped was that A.I.D. would point in the right direction, by giving the right combinations to unlock some of the doors which could not be opened by conventional survey analysis.

Four runs of the A.I.D. programme were carried out. In every case the dependent variable was unemployment length, in weeks. After a trial run and the examination of the significant variables in the earlier analysis, the following variables were chosen:

'Birthplace'; coded as 'born in survey area', 'born elsewhere'
'Country'; coded as 'born in Britain', 'born abroad'
'Age'; coded as 'under 40', '40 and over'
'Marital status'; coded in three categories 'married', 'single', and 'others'
'Different kinds of work'; the number of different kinds of work the men had done, coded as 'one', or 'more than one'
'Redundancy Pay'; coded as 'received redundancy pay from last job', 'did not receive redundancy pay'

'Mobility'; willingness to move home in search of work, coded as 'will move', 'won't move, and any other answers'

'P.D. Score'; score on the 'Personal Disturbance Scale' coded as '0–4', '5–20', with all cases where these questions were not asked being included in the 0–4 category

'Registered Occupation'; the occupation for which the men were registered at the Employment Exchanges, coded 'non-manual', 'skilled manual' and 'semi- or unskilled manual'

'Weeks sick'; weeks of recorded sickness in previous three years, coded as 'under three months', 'three months or over'

'Convictions'; number of convictions recorded for the men, coded '0', '1', '2–4', '5+'.

In the second run the same variables were used, but the men who had been unemployed over two years were excluded from the analysis. The rationale for doing this was that, at least in two of the three areas, it reduced the 'skew' in the overall distribution, to produce one that was more evely balanced around the means. This was a strategy recommended by Sonquist and Morgan (op. cit. p. 120), who suggested that in such situations extreme cases should be removed and explained separately and the analysis re-run without them. This often provides a way of securing a more refined analysis, in other words with more splits, without having to reduce standards of statistical significance. In the present study the extreme cases, in Coventry 23 men with over two years unemployment and in Hammersmith 12 such men, possessed the characteristics that will be identified for the most disadvantaged to a very marked degree. In Newcastle there were 88 men with over two years unemployment, who were much less obviously 'extreme' relative to others in the sample, making this run misleading for that area.

In the third run 'redundancy pay' and 'weeks sick' were removed from the list of variables, because of their tendency to have an impact upon the overall behaviour of the runs which was in many respects misleading. The latter was replaced by a variable known to correlate much more strongly with unemployment length, 'self-assessed disability'. The former was omitted because it was considered to mask to some degree the factors of age and skill.

In the fourth run the variables from run three were re-used with the men unemployed over two years (sometimes described below as 'the very long-term unemployed') excluded.

A.I.D. results for the Coventry sample

In all four analyses age was the first discriminator, with the young, of course, having markedly shorter unemployment (a mean of 31 weeks against 53 weeks when all the sample was included). In the following discussion, therefore, the findings for the under forties and for the over forties will be described separately.

(a) *The Under Forties*

The pattern of relationships for this group remained little changed by variations in the variables used. This meant that the various sickness measures discriminated poorly for the young group, and so did receipt or non-receipt of redundancy pay. The findings from both the analyses including all the sample, regardless of unemployment length, are presented in Figure 6.1.

Figure 6.1.

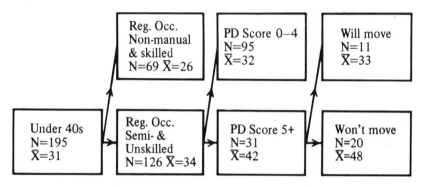

Note: In this and all subsequent charts the means ($\overline{X}$s) are expressed to the nearest week

    The most advantaged groups are those registered for non-manual or skilled work; the least advantaged are those registered for low skilled work, with P.D. scores of 5 or more, and unprepared to move.

    The two most advantaged groups, the non-manual and skilled workers and the less skilled workers with low P.D. scores, contain fairly large numbers, 69 and 95. The fact that they did not break down further means that there were no variables in the analysis which discriminated to any marked extent between those with different unemployment lengths in those two groups.

    When those with over two years unemployment were removed from the

113

Coventry sample its total size was reduced by 23, but the under 40 group was only lowered by three. The only change this made to the two charts was that the last discriminator became birthplace instead of 'mobility', with those born outside the survey area having a lower mean (33) and an N of 15. It seems likely that birthplace and mobility — having moved in the past, and being willing to move in the future — are highly inter-correlated for this group. Otherwise 'registered occupation' and 'P.D. score' remained the key discriminating variables for this group of men.

(b) *The Over Forties*

The changes made in the variables used in the analysis had a marked impact upon the results for this group. Hence it is necessary to present the findings for each run of the programme, designating the runs by Roman numerals in the order they were described above.

In run (i) 'redundancy pay' was the first variable to come out after age, with those who received it remaining out of work for a shorter time than those who did not. This conflicts with the earlier finding on this, but only because in this case the impact of age is taken into account properly. It was only the over 40s who received substantial amounts of redundancy pay. The findings on the lower unemployment of the recipients of redundancy pay appear to provide a contradiction of the hypothesis that redundancy pay acts as a disincentive to job seeking. It must be pointed out, however, that men who receive redundancy pay have in general better employment records than those who do not, so that this may affect their attractiveness to future employers.

Amongst those who received redundancy pay two groups appeared markedly advantaged, those born overseas and British born non-manual workers. The lower unemployment rate of the overseas born may be attributed to a greater willingness to move or accept employment conditions uncongenial to British born workers; there may also be a concealed age factor here, as they may be nearer to 40 than the British born. Figure 6.2 shows some of the findings for those relatively advantaged groups amongst the over 40s.

In run (i) the group shown to be most disadvantaged were those who had not received redundancy pay, were not prepared to move in order to obtain work, and were born in Coventry. They had a mean of 100 weeks. There were only 15 in this group, but there were 47 with a mean of 74 weeks in the preceding group (no redundancy pay, not prepared to move).

It is interesting that such apparently subjective factors distinguish these long-term unemployed men amongst the over 40s in Coventry. However, there is some association between willingness to move and age. There may, too, be an association between this factor and occupation or pay, since it has been

114

Figure 6.2.

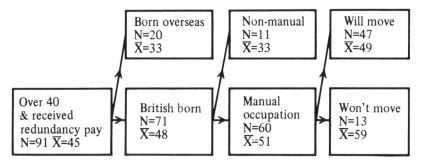

shown that many low skilled and poorly paid workers in Coventry are adequately housed in local authority property; such people have a great deal to lose from moving.

When, for run (ii), the very long-term unemployed were removed from the sample, 'registered occupation' replaced 'redundancy pay' as the main variable after age for the over 40s, with the non-manual and skilled workers having significantly shorter unemployment than the rest. The most advantaged group became the men registered for non-manual or skilled work who had no criminal records. Their mean was 33 ($N = 33$). The most disadvantaged were unskilled workers who had not received redundancy pay and who had criminal records. Their mean was 66 weeks ($N = 14$), a very high one when it is remembered that the maximum possible for the sample in this run was 104. It is interesting that criminal record appeared as a significant discriminator for the over 40s amongst both the skilled and the unskilled when the small number of very long-term unemployed men were removed from consideration.

When the changes in the variables were made for run (iii) a factor that had not figured before appeared as important, marital status. In this run the advantaged group amongst the over 40s was seen to be men who were not single, were born overseas, and were prepared to move to get work. This group had a mean of only 31 weeks ($N = 19$). The most disadvantaged were the single men who had been born in Coventry, with a mean of 85 weeks ($N = 11$). The evidence here on the vulnerable position of the elderly single supports the finding from the earlier analysis, which then only received strong support from the Hammersmith sample.

Of course, the Coventry born single and the married immigrants are two rather small sub-groups from the sample as a whole. For the large number of over 40s who were British born and married or formerly married (112) the key discriminating variable was the new one introduced in run (iii), self-assessed

115

disability. Then amongst the non-disabled, registered occupation proved to be a significant discriminator, producing the interesting doubled-barrelled breakdown shown on the upper part of Figure 6.3.

Figure 6.3.

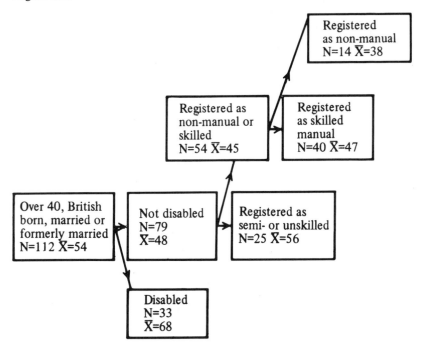

The hierarchy of 'skill' shown above is interesting, and may be contrasted with the rather different pattern shown in the Hammersmith analyses below. The disabled appear here as a fairly markedly disadvantaged group, but their mean (68 weeks) was no more than that of all the single men in this age group; this indicates the significance of single status here.

In run (iv) the impact of removing the very long-term unemployed from the analysis was to reduce the importance of marital status and increase the impact of registered occupation.

(c) *Summary*

In Coventry age is clearly the key discriminating factor. Registered occupation appears as next in order of importance. The lack of total clarity on this point as far as the over 40s are concerned seems due to a tendency for registered occupation to be a less significant factor for the very long-term unemployed. For these men personal factors, which it is not possible to isolate fully, but which seem to be associated with single status and immobility, appear to be of more importance. In other words age and skill are the key correlates of long-term unemployment, but in an area where unemployment over two years is a rarity, personal factors which can only be guessed at from these data account for exceptionally long spells out of work.

Amongst the young the P.D. score was an important discriminator; while amongst the over 40s 'redundancy pay' was significant, implying, as was suggested, a 'work-record' discriminator. Apart from those implied by the 'P.D. scale' health factors did not seem particularly salient in Coventry.

Other interesting variables in this analysis were 'mobility', 'birthplace', and 'criminality', all of which tended to figure as discriminators. Country of origin also appeared as a discriminator, with immigrants doing better than non-immigrants.

A.I.D. results for the Hammersmith sample

Once again, with age the first discriminator in every run, it is appropriate to consider the two age groups separately. The mean number of weeks of unemployment for the under 40s was 23, for the over 40s, 49.

(a) *The Under Forties*

As in Coventry the two runs including all the sample yielded similar results for this group, with neither of the sickness variables having any impact as discriminators. The pattern obtained by the two runs is set out in Figure 6.4.

This does not provide very much insight into the employment problems of this part of the sample. It looks as if the foreign born suffer as a discriminated-against group, and, unlike those in Coventry, their greater flexibility does not counter-balance this. On the other hand, amongst the British born it looks as if a factor like greater resourcefulness distinguishes those born outside London from the London born.

When the group of 12 men with uemployment over two years were removed from the sample, despite the fact that none of these were under 40, other factors appeared in the analysis, due to the reduction of the overall variance. Two of the three 'terminal' groups in the analysis mapped above were broken down further by the variable 'registered occupation'. The foreign born were split into those registered for skilled manual work, with a mean of 22 weeks

117

Figure 6.4.

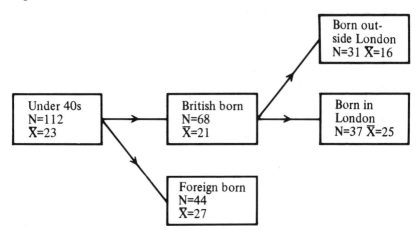

unemployment ($N = 11$), and those registered for either non-manual work or low skilled work, with a mean of 29 ($N = 33$). By contrast, the other 'split' was for the London born, amongst whom those registered for non-manual work were more advantaged with a mean of 20 ($N = 10$), as against one of 27 ($N = 27$) for manual workers. This contrast between immigrant and non-immigrant non-manual workers provides further evidence of the impact of discrimination, which is likely to fall most heavily upon this group of workers.

(b) *The Over Forties*

As in Coventry the four different runs of the A.I.D. programme each yielded rather different results for the over 40s.

   In run (i) those who were apparently in the most advantaged group amongst the over 40s were men who were prepared to move and who scored over 5 on the P.D. scale. Their mean unemployment length was 29 weeks ($N = 16$), as against a mean of 49 weeks for the age group as a whole. This result supports the theory advanced in Chapter 3 to account for the finding of a significant relationship between high P.D. score and low unemployment for the 25–49s in Hammersmith. This was that men in this category 'drift' from place to place and do not remain consistently on the unemployed register. This combination of willingness to move and high P.D. score is therefore particularly significant.

   Amongst the low P.D. scorers who were prepared to move, the most advantaged group were those born outside London. The most disadvantaged group suggested by run (i) were single men who were unprepared to move. The average

118

length of unemployment for this small group was remarkably high for Hammersmith, 86 weeks. The P.D. scores of the elderly single group were examined and 41% were found to have scored over 5, as opposed to 30% for the Hammersmith sample as a whole.

The main findings for the over 40s from the first run are set out in Figure 6.5.

Figure 6.5.

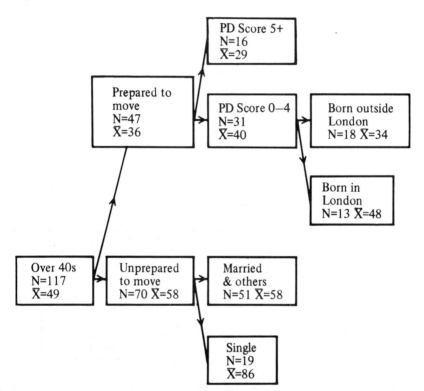

Removing the men unemployed over two years from the sample for run (ii) did not make a substantial difference to the pattern of variables for the Hammersmith over 40s. The most disadvantaged group remained the single men who were unprepared to move. On the other hand registered occupation became an important factor for some of the other groups, so that one of the most advantaged groups was men who were prepared to move and were manual workers, with a mean of 29 weeks ($N = 33$). Those amongst them with P.D. scores over 5 had a mean of 26 weeks ($N = 14$).

The change in sickness measure for run (iii) led to quite a considerable change in the pattern of variables for the older Hammersmith group. Self-ascribed disability was the most important factor after age in this run. The most advantaged group were those not disabled, prepared to move, and with manual registered occupations. They had a mean of 24 weeks unemployment ($N = 19$). The most disadvantaged group were the disabled single, with the highest mean for any group in the four Hammersmith runs, one of 96 ($N = 11$).

The effect of eliminating the very long-term unemployed for the fourth run was to remove many of the individuals in the very highly disadvantaged disabled single group. So, while disability remained the second factor after age, the remaining factors in the most disadvantaged 'tree' were as set out in Figure 6.6.

Figure 6.6.

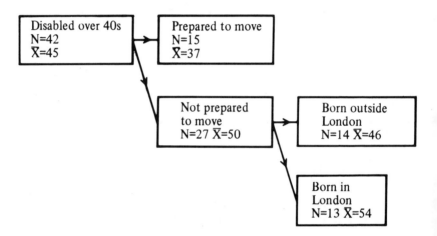

Again, this coincidence of the two mobility variables suggests some but partially tapped motivational factors.

On the fourth run only one change occurred in the pattern of variables following the category 'not-disabled' in the 'tree'. This however was interesting. Country of birth now appeared as a discriminator for the immobile, ever married, non-disabled, with the foreign born having a higher mean, 46 as against 35. This is a small piece of further evidence on the employment problems of immigrants in Hammersmith.

120

(c) *Summary*

Again age has been shown to be the most important discriminating factor. Then amongst the younger group of men place of birth is the most important determinant of employment potential, with the foreign born doing worst and the British, born outside of London, doing best. The differences are overall very slight, however. Exclusion of the very long unemployed from the Hammersmith distribution has the effect of making one more variable appear significant for the under 40s, registered occupation.

In the initial analysis for the men over 40 willingness to move and marital status appeared as the key factors. When the 'sickness indicator' was changed to 'self-assessed disability' this appeared as the most important factor after age. The health variables were not significant discriminators for the under 40s.

It was reported earlier that when using ordinary cross-tabulation techniques, occupation did not appear as a good unemployment predictor in Hammersmith. The A.I.D. results substantiate this, but throw a little more light on why Hammersmith differs from the other two areas. Firstly, registered occupation does not feature as one of the primary variables in determining unemployment potential. Secondly, when it does appear in the analysis it is seen to have an unusual impact as compared with the other areas. In the immigrant group the skilled workers do better, while for the older men non-manual workers are shown to be relatively more disadvantaged than the manual workers.

The A.I.D. analysis brought out very clearly the disadvantaged position of the elderly single in Hammersmith. It also provided further confirmation of the difficulty of isolating special problem groups in Hammersmith, with high P.D. scores again appearing as apparent predictors of good employment prospects, and the criminal record variables failing to operate as effective discriminators.

A.I.D. results for the Newcastle sample

In one sense the A.I D. findings for Newcastle were very straightforward, the 'big three' variables – age, registered occupation, and self-assessed disability – coming through clearly as the main determinants of unemployment length. In another sense the A.I.D. programme was difficult to use for the Newcastle data. Three things made it so: (a) the overwhelming importance of the major variables tended to render the other variables poor and inconsistent discriminators. (b) As explained earlier, the elimination of men with over two years' unemployment from the sample, which proved so revealing for the analyses in the other two areas, had too drastic an effect in Newcastle. These runs of the programme are therefore not described, as it makes little sense to talk about

121

relative disadvantage with a substantial number of the really disadvantaged excluded from the analysis. (c) At the same time the effect of the inclusion of men who had been unemployed for the whole of the review period made the sickness variable, 'weeks sick', behave in a misleading way and upset much of the first run. The reasons for the misleading behaviour of this variable were discussed on p. 49.

The impact of the three major variables can best be described by setting out the major advantaged and disadvantaged groups as shown by the first part of the run (iii) (see Figure 6.7).

In the above figure the over 40s and the under 40s have been shown together. It is revealing to do this as (a) the basic 'trees' are identical, and (b) the contrasts are so dramatic. Age is obviously a very powerful discriminating variable, yet those amongst the over 40s registered for non-manual or skilled work did nearly as well as the under 40s as a whole, while those amongst the under 40s who were registered for semi- or unskilled work and who were disabled did almost as badly as the over 40s as a whole. When all three variables are taken together the gap between the mean of the most advantaged group (under 40s registered for non-manual work or skilled work) and the most disadvantaged group (disabled over 40s registered for semi- or unskilled work) is enormous, 86 weeks. Finally, it is interesting to note that the variable 'disability' does not discriminate within the non-manual and skilled groups.

(a) *The Under Forties*

Although the basic picture for Newcastle has already been described, it is helpful to follow the procedure adopted in the sections on the other areas, to describe the impact of other factors in relation to the two separate age groups. On the run described above, both the non-manual and skilled group and the disabled group were 'terminal' groups, that is no further variable was present that would significantly discriminate between men. The other group, 'the not disabled unskilled' were next split into a more advantaged group born outside Newcastle, with a mean of 39 ($N = 41$) and a less advantaged group born in Newcastle, with a mean of 56 ($N = 90$). The latter could be split again by 'convictions', but in a surprising way, with those with five or more convictions doing better (mean of 45, N of 30) than those with 0–4 (Mean of 60, N of 61). This is hard to explain, except in terms of the weakness of the dependent variable 'unemployment length' for certain specific sub-groups which was suggested earlier (see p. 51), unless it is the case that in this poor labour market the ex-criminals are more resourceful?

On the first run, where the strong sickness discriminator, disability, was

Figure 6.7.

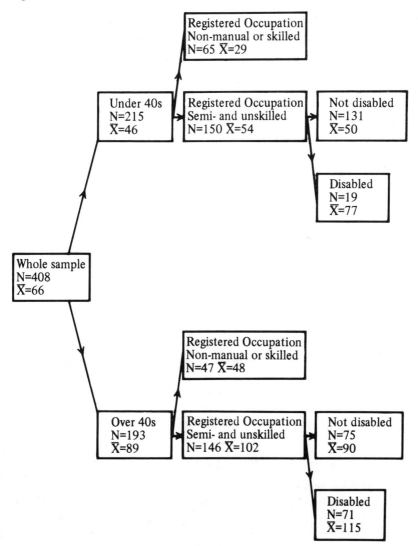

missing from the analysis the pattern was much the same, apart from the fact that 'birthplace' was in the place taken by disability in the run (iii) as the main discriminator for the low skilled group. This was followed by 'weeks sick' operating in the distorting way described above.

(b) *The Over Forties*

As with the under 40s in run (iii), no further variable split the non-manual
and skilled over 40s. The two other groups in the diagram above were however
both next divided in rather surprising ways. For the non-disabled unskilled,
P.D. score was the next discriminator, but it split this group into a group of
10 with a mean of 58 who scored 5 or more on the P.D. scale and a group of
65 with a mean of 94 who scored 4 or below. What makes this particularly
surprising is the earlier reported findings on the way in which high P.D. scores
were significantly associated with long unemployment in Newcastle. However,
there is no need to worry unduly about this very small sub-group, whose mean
may have been lowered by the hospitalization of some of them. The low P.D.
scorers next 'split' in the way shown in Figure 6.8.

Figure 6.8.

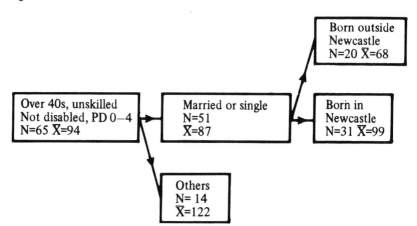

Figure 6.8.is peripherally interesting for isolating one more small disadvantaged group — the widowed, separated or divorced elderly, not disabled, unskilled
workers — and for suggesting that even amongst the severely disadvantaged
elderly low-skilled in Newcastle, the variable 'birthplace', which has been assumed
to imply motivational factors of some kind, has a quite marked impact.

The low skilled disabled over 40s were also further 'split' several times,
though these have little significance as the mean of this group was so enormous.
In other words, a distinction between a group of men with an average of 2
years unemployment and one with 2½ years is bound to be comparatively
meaningless, with chance factors having a more than usually large impact.
124

On the first run registered occupation was also the first discriminator after age, but then the value of the rest of the 'tree' was largely undermined by a division of the low skilled on the variable 'weeks sick', with those with no sickness having most unemployment, so there is little point in reporting the findings further.

(c) *Conclusion*

In concluding this discussion of Newcastle it is not necessary to do much more than reiterate the importance of age, registered occupation and self-assessed disability. Beyond the enormous impact of these three, however, it was interesting to see that 'elusive' variable 'birthplace' figuring significantly.

In Newcastle, no clear evidence was provided to support the findings from Coventry and Hammersmith on the disadvantaged elderly single. However, there were very few elderly single in the Newcastle sample and it is therefore significant that some evidence was provided on the disadvantaged position of the most comparable group, the formerly married.

It is also worthy of note that criminal record appeared in the 'tree' for the younger men in Newcastle as a factor associated with short unemployment. It also appeared in the same way on the unreported 'tree' for the elderly low skilled disabled.

Conclusions

At one level the findings would not appear to improve upon relatively informed general knowledge, since the results of the research indicate that the three crucial variables determining unemployment length are age, skill and health. This can be justified on the scientific grounds that evidence of the 'obvious' is needed and that it is necessary to eliminate the obvious in order to see the not so obvious. In the first place, while age, skill, and health were found to be the major variables, with more detailed scrutiny it was revealed that they did not 'behave' in a way which accorded with conventional wisdom. The major variables had a quite different impact in different groups and different areas. This was particularly apparent in Hammersmith, where skill, as defined by registered occupation, did not really feature as a major variable, and when it did feature exerted influence in a fashion quite different to that in other areas and in a way which differed from what might be regarded as obvious.

The importance of age has been clearly demonstrated, yet at the margin skill can offset the effects of age. However, the A.I.D. analysis showed that age was always the first characteristic to discriminate, and that on the basis of age alone, a man aged over 40 years is likely to suffer longer unemployment.

Registered occupation was the second most important factor in both New-castle and Coventry, but not in Hammersmith, where its impact was blunted by other factors, such as birthplace and willingness to move.

Health was the third most important factor in Newcastle for men both over and under 40. In Hammersmith, on the other hand, it was only a significant factor for older men, while in Coventry – where a much smaller proportion of the sample claimed to be disabled – its impact seemed to be fairly minimal, particularly for the young.

Mental health, as measured by the Personal Disturbance Scale, did appear as a clearly important factor for the younger men in Coventry. However, it still showed its impact to be problematic, as had been discovered earlier, in Hammersmith. The A.I.D. programme also suggested that its impact in New-castle was less obvious than had earlier been believed.

One of the more original products of the A.I.D. analysis was to highlight the importance of two variables which had not previously been identified as prominent, namely birthplace and mobility. Of the two, birthplace showed itself to be of particular importance in all areas. These two factors were quite probably indirect indicators of motivation.

Beyond the main variables the picture in every area was quite different and there seems little point in repeating the most advantaged and disadvantaged groups within each area. There is one group of particularly disadvantaged men who are worthy of special note and these are the elderly single in both Hammer-smith and Coventry. They were shown to be disadvantaged in the earlier analysis but the A.I.D. analysis emphasised their predicament in a particularly striking manner. It is clear that the group are worthy of further study.

The large number of men in receipt of redundancy pay in Coventry gave a good opportunity to study any possible effects. The results with A.I.D. in Coventry would seem to indicate that there is no evidence from that area to support the hypothesis that redundancy pay has a major impact in deterring men from returning to work.

Finally, it is worthwhile to relate the profiles of long-term unemployment in the three areas, as provided by the A.I.D. programme, to what is known of the economic causes of unemployment.

Newcastle has had an above average level of unemployment for a very long period. It may be described as a place which is close to economic stagnation, despite some of the more conspicuous changes which have altered the look of the city centre. It might be expected from the general weakness of the economy in this area, and the structural changes which ushered in the area's decline, that unemployment would be suffered by a wide range of people in Newcastle. However, it may be suggested that the effect of persistent unemployment has been to sort out the labour force in such a way that the long-term unemployed can be very clearly identified as those who are least attractive to employers the world over – the elderly, the low skilled and the disabled. Clearly, as heavy industry has declined in the Newcastle area and new employment has come mainly as a result of expansion in the service industries, manual workers with little skill have continued to find it very difficult to get work. It is significant, therefore, that, according to the A.I.D. findings, even within the severely disadvantaged elderly group those registered for non-manual and skilled work stand out as having above average prospects of getting work, while the young unskilled are almost as disadvantaged as the over forties. The tendency for the middle-aged and elderly unskilled to form a 'hard core' whose prospects are very grim indeed will have been further highlighted by the tendency for other less disadvantaged workers to leave the district when faced by employment problems.

Hammersmith is in many respects the extreme opposite of Newcastle. Employees do not remain out of work long there, and much of the unemployment in that area may be described as 'frictional', due to minor inefficiency in the way the labour market works as men move between jobs. There seems to be plenty of low skilled work there, as skill does not figure very much as a correlate of long-term unemployment. The groups who suffer most unemployment are those who experience some degree of discrimination from employers, the elderly (particularly if disabled) and the immigrants, for example. The individuals who are often expected to have poor employment prospects on grounds of personal 'pathology', the mentally ill and those with criminal records, probably do not find it hard to get work in this area, but they may be identified as individuals who do not hold jobs for very long. Some more detailed work on the correlates of such employment patterns will be reported in the second book on this survey.

The Coventry situation is a little more difficult to explain. During 1971 the labour market worsened fairly dramatically there for manual workers. Few of the unemployed were non-manual workers, but the skilled manual workers were quite significantly represented amongst the unemployed in October 1971. However, these skilled men seem to have had much less difficulty than the unskilled in getting back into work. Thus skill figured as the major discriminator after age, according to the A.I.D. programme. What is more difficult to explain is why the disabled do not show up as a disadvantaged group in Coventry. It has been reported that the disabled were a fairly small element amongst Coventry's unemployed. This does not, on the face of it, provide any reason why the disabled do not appear as proportionately more disadvantaged. Yet it must be considered that in a younger and fitter population (the comparison here is particularly between Coventry and Newcastle) it is rather easier for the industrial system to provide suitable places for a small disabled group. In as much, furthermore, as the Department of Employment is successful in enforcing the 'quota' system, which reserves a proportion of each firm's labour force for the disabled, a small disabled population will obviously fare better than a large one.

Another difference to be explained is the A.I.D. finding that immigrants from overseas in Coventry did relatively better than the native population, while in Hammersmith they did relatively worse. In Coventry skill proved to be a strong discriminator; the overseas born within the unskilled were shown to have a tendency towards shorter unemployment. It may be suggested that discrimination is relatively slight for low skilled workers (see W.W. Daniel) and that flexibility and readiness to take any kind of work on the part of the large Asian element in the Coventry overseas born will have accounted for greater success here. In Hammersmith, on the other hand, the finding that place of birth was a more significant variable than skill, for the under 40s, was likely to mean that the greater disadvantages faced by the foreign born as a group were a combination of the generally slightly poorer employment prospects of the low skilled, who were prominent in that group, together with the impact of discrimination against immigrant white collar workers, who were shown in the next stage of the A.I.D. analysis to be a significantly disadvantaged group.

The A.I.D. analysis provided, particularly then, a means of highlighting the differences in the characteristics of the employment situations in the three areas studied. It helped to impose some order on a group of findings which were often difficult to relate to each other. It generated, too, some hypotheses; some of which must await other students of this subject. Others will be further tested in the later analysis of this study to be reported in the second book.

7 Discussion of the findings

Introduction

In this chapter the more important findings will be drawn together and considered in relation to the hypotheses and arguments set out in the first chapter. It should be remembered that this research was of an exploratory nature, aiming to identify the main characteristics of unemployed men, and particularly of men who might be regarded as long-term or chronic unemployed. Theories about long-term unemployment, where it is not in any simple way attributable to obvious economic factors, were seen as falling into two main groups, those which explained it in terms of the low motivation of certain individuals and those which drew attention to the unattractiveness of long-term unemployed men to potential employers. At the same time it was believed that these two different kinds of explanation are not in practice likely to be so separate, and that in any case neither could be considered without reference to broader economic factors. Certain characteristics become employment handicaps as a function of the level of economic activity and local labour market conditions, rather than acting as independent variables in the economic situation.

Motivation and 'Voluntary Unemployment'

The first part of this chapter will deal with the evidence for explanations of unemployment in terms of motivation, and thus, in some senses, with the phenomenon which is often portrayed as voluntary unemployment. In the first chapter it was made clear that in any absolute form propositions about voluntary unemployment are not amenable to scientific testing. It is necessary, here, to add to that observation a further warning on the interpretation of the data presented in this book. The broad social characteristics of the long-term unemployed have been clearly identified, but only in terms of statistical probabilities. It should not be assumed that anyone whose unemployment cannot be 'explained' by his membership of a disadvantaged statistical group is therefore voluntarily unemployed. It cannot, for example, be concluded that, because skill did not appear to be very strongly associated with employment difficulties in Hammersmith, it would be unjustified for a particular individual to claim skill, or lack of it, as the basis of his unemployment problems in that particular area; or that, because even handicapped people obtain work in Hammersmith, those who are fit and able and unemployed for more than a very short period

129

of time must be voluntarily unemployed. Such logical deduction is completely spurious, since it assumes a degree of perfection which cannot be achieved by any survey. There will always be factors which are overlooked. This issue will be further discussed later in this chapter. The point to be made here, however, is that this research indicates, irrespective of whether personal or 'moral' characteristics of certain groups or individuals do prolong the periods of unemployment some may undergo, that there appear to be certain factors of a more observable nature which are quite strongly associated with prolonged unemployment, and that these factors, which are amenable to manipulation providing there is the will to do so, are more important in explaining unemployment than the moral attitudes of particular men.

Having said this, it was nevertheless possible to test some hypotheses dealing with motivational factors. First, there is the hypothesis about the importance of monetary incentives. It has been argued that some men remain unemployed because of the lack of financial incentives to go to work. For certain groups, particularly those with large families, more, or nearly as much, money may sometimes be obtained by remaining out of work as by gaining employment. From the findings presented in Chapter 4 it appears there is some association between having a larger income while unemployed and experiencing longer periods of unemployment. It should be noted, however, that these were a group of men who had exceptionally low incomes while in work, which were often the result of other characteristics which made them unattractive to employers, and were therefore also associated with longer periods of unemployment. It was further concluded that the small group of men with out of work incomes above either their past earnings or their future expected earnings were often men with other sources of income, such as Family Allowances or wife's earnings, which would continue once they returned to work. It should also be pointed out that several of them would qualify for Family Income Supplement, a new benefit remaining in payment when men are in full time work, which had been introduced only about two months before the survey was conducted.

There seems to be no evidence from this survey to substantiate the view that many men remain unemployed because it is more lucrative than working. It is very doubtful that more than a very small number of men fall into this category, and secondly, it cannot be conclusively proved that longer periods of unemployment are due to high unemployment income, rather than the possession of other characteristics such as a low level of skill.

A similar position was found with regard to the hypothesis that large redundancy payments encourage long-term unemployment. Amongst the unemployed as a whole men who received redundancy pay did appear to remain out of work for longer periods. However, when age was held constant
130

this relationship did not remain. In fact the A.I.D. analysis indicated that after the effects of age had been taken into account the recipients of redundancy pay were shown as experiencing on average shorter unemployment. This was attributed to the possession of a good past employment record, which, by definition, recipients of redundancy pay must have. A good employment record is probably the most important characteristic in gaining acceptance from a new employer.

Acceptable levels of pay were inversely related to length of unemployment. Therefore, it cannot be argued that men remained out of work because they demanded rates of pay that were essentially unobtainable. Neither did they remain unemployed because they were extremely selective about the kinds of work they were prepared to do. Those who claimed to be more selective were not found to experience longer periods of unemployment, since the most selective were the more highly skilled who found it relatively easier to gain re-employment.

An indirect measure of motivation was provided by the questions about willingness to move or work away from home. There did appear to be some indication of an association between willingness to move and shorter periods of unemployment. It is a reasonable assumption that the answer to this question is an indicator of motivation, since it is very unlikely that many men, even when they indicated willingness to move, did in fact obtain jobs by leaving the area. Certainly, very few had their papers transferred to other areas by the Employment Exchanges. What was measured was more likely to be the men's willingness to undergo personal inconvenience in order to obtain work.

Just over half the samples in all three areas claimed that they were prepared to move, and there was evidence of shorter unemployment for this group. However, when age was taken into account the association only remained in Hammersmith, but there it did so for all three age groups. The same type of relationship was manifest in the A.I.D. analysis, where willingness to move was the most important unemployment predictor for men over 40 years. In Coventry willingness to move only appeared after the major variables of age, health and skill were taken into account. (See Figs. 6.1 and 6.2).

There are two difficulties, therefore, with this finding. The first is that the techniques to 'hold age constant' involved breaking the samples up into fairly large age groups. It may have been the case, then, that unwillingness to move was associated with greater age within any specific age group. This suspicion is reinforced by the fact that in the A.I.D. analysis it was amongst the over 40s, an age group stretching up to 65, that unwillingness to move was associated with longer unemployment.

The other difficulty with the finding is that what was measured may not have been a 'cause' of prolonged unemployment but an effect of it. The

131

demoralising effects of long unemployment have been commonly reported (Bakke; Jahoda et al) and unwillingness to consider moving is a fairly obvious symptom of this phenomenon.

The evidence in relation to job hunting, which might also be regarded as a measure of motivation, indicated no differences in length of unemployment, nor did the intensity (number of methods used to seek work) with which work was sought, except in relation to the more extreme unemployment lengths of over two years, where again the demoralisation theory is relevant.

In general, then, the evidence provided by this survey on the significance of motivation is very weak. The strongest evidence came from the Hammersmith sample, and there is therefore some justification in arguing that unless employment can be raised in all areas to a level which is the same as that found in Hammersmith, there is little point in being concerned about motivation. If motivation is to be accepted as an important factor it can only be so when unemployment is at a low level, and in no way can it be seen to account for the present high levels of unemployment.

The Main Characteristics of the Long-Term Unemployed

Both the conventional and the more sophisticated statistical analysis indicated that unquestionably in all three areas age was the most important characteristic in relation to length of unemployment. However, there did appear to be a crucial threshold, which for two areas, Coventry and Newcastle, was 40 years, while in Hammersmith it was 50 years. Age is, of course, associated with diminishing health and possible diminishing work capacity, but it may be doubted whether this alone accounts for the discrimination experienced by these older workers when attempting to gain re-employment. It was significant, too, that the younger men in the samples had changed jobs much more frequently than the older men during the previous three years. Clearly few of them had problems in getting jobs, even if they had difficulties in finding a settled place in the employment structure. It might be argued that these findings provide evidence to support the view that there is some degree of irrational discrimination against older workers, for, in spite of their lesser stability, employers still show a preference for younger men. However before arriving at this conclusion there is a need to consider whether there is some evidence here for the dual labour market hypothesis (see Hall; Bosanquet and Doeringer), with the younger men going to jobs in that insecure part of the market where employers are content with a transitory exchange of money for muscle, while the older men are interested in employment in rather more secure jobs. Clearly if such a situation exists, then the problem for the low skilled young will be insecure and unsatisfactory employment, while for the elderly a serious situation

132

exists once a secure niche in the labour force is lost for any reason. In addition, as the findings of this research seem to indicate, particularly chronic problems will be faced by low skilled men who fail to move into more stable employment before their increasing years reduce their attractiveness to the kind of employers who care little about stability, but simply assess men in terms of their physique.

The possession of a disability, as perceived by the men, was very strongly associated with unemployment even when age was held constant. This association was strong in Newcastle and Hammersmith, and particularly strong in the latter area. There a relationship between disability and unemployment was manifest for both the under 25s and the over 50s. In Newcastle the association was only statistically significant for the group between the ages of 25 and 49 years. It is quite likely that the negative effect on employability of being over 50 years is so great in Newcastle that the possession of a disability becomes irrelevant.

There was no association between disability and unemployment in Coventry. This is not very easy to explain. There was certainly a smaller proportion of disabled men in the sample there, that is both the self-assessed and the registered disabled. This is what might be expected when there is a rapid rise in unemployment, which did occur in Coventry, in contrast to the more stable situations of Hammersmith and Newcastle. But the lower proportion of disabled does not in itself explain why they did better than elsewhere. At a time of general difficulty a group that might usually appear particularly disadvantaged are likely to appear relatively less disadvantaged, but even when this is taken into consideration it is still difficult to explain why lack of skill should feature more prominently as a predictor of unemployment than disability.

Coventry has an employment market which is dominated by a few very large employers. In 1966 two thirds of all those employed in manufacturing were in ten firms; it may be hypothesized that this makes the work of the Disablement Resettlement Officer a little easier. In conjunction with this point it should be noted that the disablement quota regulations (every firm employing over 20 people must employ 3% of disabled persons) only become effective at the point of hiring and firing. Thus there may well be a situation in which the disabled population are the last to go and amongst the first to return. An employer will have to lay off approximately 32 workers before he can reduce his disabled workers by one. On the other hand, even though he has to increase his labour force by 32 before he is compelled to take on a disabled worker, the 32 may be at any skill level. Therefore, in this situation it may be possible for the disabled workers to do better than the unskilled where there is high labour turnover, which was typical of Coventry even when there was low unemployment. Furthermore, it is very often the case that firms are below their quota of disabled workers. When such firms are discharging workers this situation may protect the disabled from redundancy, while when they are hiring workers the Department of Employment will be able relatively easily to persuade them to consider disabled men. These arguments are, however, highly speculative and it must be remembered that Coventry was being studied during an atypical period as far as unemployment was concerned.

As well as health, in terms of disability, mental health, as measured by the pre-diagnostic scale (the Personal Disturbance Scale), was seen to be of some importance, although the findings were a little problematic in nature. When age was controlled some degree of association was apparent between high P.D. score and long unemployment in Coventry and Newcastle; this association was statistically significant amongst the under 25s in Newcastle. In Hammersmith, on the other hand, the relationship between these two variables was inverse, and for the 25–49 age group that association was statistically significant. Yet, at the same time, a positive association was found in Hammersmith between high P.D. scores and frequent job changing.

There are several interesting features of the Hammersmith findings that require bringing together here. A much higher proportion of the Hammersmith sample, 30%, had significantly high P.D. scores. A higher proportion had received treatment for mental illness, too, according to the medical certificate records. There was also in the Hammersmith sample a higher proportion of single men than in the other samples; and, although in all areas single status tended to be associated with longer unemployment when age was held constant, this relationship was most marked amongst the older men in Hammersmith. This association between single status and longer unemployment may be partly attributable to the absence of pressures derived from family commitments, but it does not seem unreasonable to suggest that there are other more complex psychological factors which may be either causes or consequences of single status (or both). Single men may also possibly experience some discrimination. In Hammersmith, an area where much accommodation is available for rootless single men, and where migrants of many kinds are found, many of the unemployed were men who appeared to be facing personal psychological problems of various kinds. At the same time the wide range of work available in that area meant that these men, so long as they were young and physically fit, were rarely unemployed for long. The inconsistent nature of the findings for this group was, furthermore, reinforced by the survey's dependence on registered unemployment as a measure of unemployment, so that some men with unsettled ways of life tended misleadingly to appear to be amongst the ranks of those who returned to work quickly.

In all three areas there was an association between skill level and unemployment length; this was most marked when the measure of skill used was 'registered

134

occupation', based on the occupations which the Employment Exchanges had accepted as appropriate for the men. This association was strong, and generally statistically significant, even when other factors were taken into account, in Coventry and Newcastle. In Hammersmith, on the other hand, it was much less marked. The various skill levels were treated as a hierarchy, running from non-manual workers through skilled manual workers to unskilled manual workers. In Coventry and Newcastle the non-manual workers were comparatively few, so that the skill level comparison was largely between skilled and unskilled manual workers. In Hammersmith, on the other hand, there was a substantial non-manual group, and much of the weak association between unemployment length and skill can be explained in terms of the relatively disadvantaged position of this group of workers, particularly as compared with the skilled manual workers. The A.I.D. analysis brought out rather clearly the fact that two sub-groups within the non-manual workers, the overseas born and the elderly, figured as relatively disadvantaged.

Having qualified the Hammersmith finding in this way, it is still appropriate to point out that the low skilled men in that area were in relative terms, and certainly in absolute terms, much less disadvantaged than in the other two areas. However, as asserted, but not fully explained, earlier in the chapter, it should not be assumed that because skill is not strongly associated with unemployment in Hammersmith, a young fit unskilled worker unemployed for more than a short period must be 'voluntarily' unemployed. There are two main reasons why such a conclusion is invalid. Firstly, it assumes a degree of perfection on the part of the survey which it does not, and could not, possess. Skill appears less important but there may be a large number of related factors, which are important but are not recorded. Secondly, it makes the common error of placing all unskilled workers in one homogenous group. There is no evidence to show that because unskilled workers as a whole do not suffer disadvantage compared with other skill groups, sub-groups amongst the unskilled are equally advantaged. Within the category of unskilled work there is a great deal of dif-ferentiation and specialisation requiring men to possess past experience and knowledge. A factory labourer, for example, may find it very difficult to obtain work on a building site, and vice-versa. The findings of this research are that skill is not strongly associated with unemployment in the London borough, but there may be many factors outside the scope of the research that are associated, and until these factors are known or proved not to exist conclusions about the actual causes of unemployment amongst the young, fit unskilled workers should be made with careful reservations.

While examining skill levels in relation to unemployment it is interesting to consider the relationship between the different measures of skill used in the survey and unemployment. Skill as measured by registered occupation was undoubtedly the best of the predictors of unemployment length. It is however, rather puzzling that there were such considerable discrepancies between the different measures. Apart from registered occupation the other measures used were last job and what the respondent regarded as his usual occupation. The discrepancy between usual occupation and the other measures was least surprising. It is accepted that men may indulge in a degree of self promotion. It is more disturbing that there should be quite noticeable discrepancies between last job and registered occupation. In Coventry 38% of the men with last jobs which were skilled were registered as semi- or unskilled workers. Comparable figures for Hammersmith and Newcastle were 36% and 44%.

The policy of the Department of Employment is to classify men on the basis of what they are known to be capable of doing, rather than what they think they are capable of, or would like to do. The best method of determining this must surely be based on what the men have done in the past, and particularly their last jobs. Naturally the staff of the Employment Exchanges will examine men's work histories thoroughly so that they are not dependent solely, as the survey was, on the accounts given of last jobs, particularly when those jobs were held only for short periods. However, even when this is taken into account, the number of discrepancies between reported last jobs and registered occupations seems surprisingly large. The fact that registered occupation associates so well with unemployment length could be a vindication of the Exchanges' caution. But it may be that over-cautious classification of men's skills creates a self-fulfilling prophecy. The lower a man goes down the occupational ladder the greater the competition for jobs. For certain sub-groups, particularly the disabled, this downgrading may turn a difficult situation into an impossible one. In this respect it is striking that about 40% of all the men who claimed to be disabled, and whose last job was skilled, were downgraded. This could have been tantamount to labelling these men as rejects. It is worth noting that two frequently expressed criticisms of the Exchange from those dissatisfied with its services were (1) failure to take account of previous job experience and (2) failure to take account of job preferences.

These findings are also important in relation to the findings of research into the operation of the labour market (Mackay et al), as well as the Department of Employment's assessment of its own difficulties. For it would appear that an important failing of the Employment Exchanges, from the point of view of both the employers and employees, is an inadequency in handling vacancies for skilled work. The employers feel that the Exchanges are not very good at finding skilled personnel, while skilled workers do not feel Exchanges are very good at supplying jobs for skilled men. The Department of Employment see themselves as stigmatised because they deal mainly with unskilled unemployed workers.

136

The vicious circle between the employers, employees and the Exchanges will not easily be broken, but the logic of the present situation suggests that the most fruitful way out is to attempt to maximise the employment potential, through guidance and training, of this large group of men who currently appear to be, or feel themselves to be, downgraded by the Department of Employment. It also suggests that one contemporary development in the employment services, the adoption of an 'open' system of information on job vacancies, so that men can go for jobs without having first to get the approval of Exchange officials, may make things easier for these 'marginal' skilled men.

Both Coventry and Hammersmith had quite substantial populations of immigrants from the 'new', or 'black', Commonwealth, and although the numbers within the respective samples were not sufficiently large to enable much very sophisticated analysis, it was possible to gain some insight into the unemployment problems of these groups. When the appropriate controls were made, so that like could be compared with like in terms of age and skill, there was a tendency in Hammersmith, but not in Coventry, for the black immigrant workers to do slightly worse. The A.I.D. analysis suggested that amongst the under 40s in Hammersmith 'ethnicity' was the most important influence upon employment prospects. The occupational group who 'did best' amongst these immigrants were men registered for skilled work, for whom, it may be hypothesized, the relative abundance of vacancies reduced the impact of discrimination.

In Coventry, on the other hand, the A.I.D. analysis indicated that the black workers under the age of 40 years did slightly better than their British counterparts. It is only possible to conjecture on why this may have been so. It could be that Coventry, a relatively modern city with better quality houses and other social amenities, is more tolerant. It may be that Coventry's immigrant workers have settled in that particular city because the prospects for the type of work they seek are especially good. A third possible explanation lies in the fact that the immigrant population of Coventry was predominantly Asian, whereas in Hammersmith it was predominantly West Indian. It is conceivable that there are differences in the degree of discrimination exercised against certain ethnic groups, or in the extent to which different groups are prepared to accept any kind of work. On this last point, it may be that West Indians, as a less recent and more anglicised group of immigrants, may be less prepared to consider vacancies in the 'secondary' labour market described earlier, and will therefore be more likely to be competing for jobs where both levels of competition and levels of discrimination are likely to be higher.

Straightforward tabulations did not indicate any statistically significant associations between internal migration and unemployment length, but there was some slight indication of advantage for those born outside the survey areas.

137

This was supported by analysis conducted with the A.I.D. programme.

Accepting that there is some advantage for those born outside the locality in which they work, this may be explained firstly in terms of greater motivation. But it is necessary to judge this argument in the light of the evidence presented above in connection with job seeking. Secondly, people may have tended to move to areas where the prospects for the type of work they were seeking were particularly good.

The possession of a criminal record has been hypothesized to be a characteristic that will lead to discrimination by employers, and another indirect indicator of the possession of personality characteristics which may be linked with motivational problems in relation to the securing and keeping of jobs. Some more detailed analysis might have been done to try to distinguish these interpretations of the employment problems of men with criminal records, if the survey had yielded any substantial amount of significant evidence of an association between possession of a criminal record and length of unemployment. The scanty findings from this survey on that subject should not be taken as a satisfactory refutation of the hypothesis that such men are more prone to difficulties in getting work. This is, first, because the measure of unemployment length used was likely to be unreliable for those within the group with criminal records, who remained on the margins of the officially recognised world, in which a clear line could be drawn between insured work and registered unemployment. With the small numbers of men with 'records' in the samples it only needed a few people of this kind to destroy the possibility of perceiving any clear statistical associations. Second, the officially sponsored nature of the research, with a sample drawn from employment records and warned by means of a 'ministerial' letter, was likely to have deterred some ex-criminals from co-operating. Third, a very large sample would have been necessary to provide a sufficient range of men with recent and relevant criminal records to make it possible to relate their experiences in any sophisticated way to others in comparable situations but without such records, or to distinguish offences of a serious nature. Thus, it was significant that quite a large proportion of the men in the Newcastle sample had 'records', but the great majority of these were relatively old ones relating to minor offences. It is hoped, therefore, that the inconclusive nature of the findings in this survey on the significance of criminal records will serve to warn future researchers, who want to go more deeply into this issue, of some of the difficulties involved.

Poverty and Deprivation amongst the Unemployed

One hypothesis with which the research was concerned suggested that unemployment would be but a part of a more general problem of social handicap or

138

underprivilege. This was one of the main reasons for a survey covering such a wide range of topics, including the housing situations of the sample. The findings on housing, however, did not support the hypothesis. Local authority housing provided an important source of good housing for a substantial segment of each sample, and raised the general levels of housing accommodation above those prevailing in each area. There was some tendency for the nature and quality of accommodation to be related to income and occupation, as might be expected, but the cross-cutting impact of local authority provision obscured any clear relation that there might have been. It is worthy of note that the area with the most favourable employment prospects, namely Hammersmith, is the one in which the worst housing conditions were found.

There is little question that the majority of the unemployed were living, at the time they were selected for the sample, on what can be described as no more than subsistence incomes. In each area around two-thirds had incomes of less than £15 per week, while only about a sixth had over £20 per week. Average manual worker earnings in each area were substantially above this level. For most of them social security benefits, unemployment benefit and supplementary benefits were the main sources of income. 29% in Coventry, 17% in Hammersmith and 8% in Newcastle, plus a small number more in each area who refused to acknowledge the fact, had received redundancy pay when they lost their last jobs. For a minority of this group, the sum received was quite substantial. However most of those benefitting to any degree from the redundancy pay scheme were elderly, and it has already been made quite clear that age is the prime 'determinant' of long unemployment, so it may be concluded that the extent to which this source of aid mitigated poverty amongst the unemployed was quite limited.

At the extreme end of the poverty scale it was shown, on the basis of a series of very cautious assumptions, that there was a small group of unemployed men whose incomes in the week ending 1 October 1971 fell seriously below the minimum levels prescribed by the Supplementary Benefits Commission. The authors have little doubt that these findings occurred as a consequence of the inefficiency of a system of relief in which individuals' incomes are highly dependent upon (a) their making specific applications for means-tested aid, and (b) their need to keep the S.B.C. staff informed on changes in their circumstances to ensure the continuance of that aid at the right level.

The unemployed are often considered to be amongst the 'less deserving poor'. Public sympathy is more readily aroused for the needs of the old or the sick, while the unemployed are regarded as people who will be readily removed from the ranks of the poor by return to work. There are some important points to be made about the poverty of the long-term unemployed. In as much as many of the unemployed are elderly and disabled, it is important to acknowledge that the distinction between, on the one hand, age and sickness and, on the other, unemployment as a cause of poverty is in many cases a narrow one. Many of the elderly unemployed are in practice 'pensioners' who have been forced to retire early, while the disabled men on the unemployment registers are sometimes only there because they refuse to give up hope of getting work and join the 'sick list'.Another feature of the unemployed, and particularly of the long-term unemployed, is, as has already been stressed, their low earning potential. For such people, seriously deficient incomes out of work cannot be balanced by high rewards in work. Overall, less than a fifth of the men in the samples expected to get incomes in work that would reasonably compare with the average earnings of manual workers in their areas.

The Relation between Social and Economic 'Causes' of Unemployment

At the beginning of the chapter reference was made to the argument in the first chapter, that there are considerable logical difficulties to be encountered in attempting to distinguish those 'causes' of unemployment which may be said to be related to the social or psychological characteristics of individuals from the economic 'causes'. This study has not really succeeded in overcoming these difficulties; for what it has shown has been that in a situation of high unemployment the main sufferers from long-term unemployment are men possessing characteristics which it is fairly self-evident will make them unattractive to employers.

In both Newcastle and Coventry it was very clear that elderly men, men with little skill, and, to some extent, men with disabilities were prone to very long periods of unemployment. In Hammersmith, on the other hand, these factors were less clearly important; and, in any case, vulnerable groups in that area tended to suffer very much shorter spells of unemployment than in the other two areas. This provides evidence for the general argument about the relationship between economic and social causes developed by Beveridge early in this century. His general view was quoted in the first chapter, but equally he showed a clear awareness of the relativity of the concepts used in relation to unemployability. He argued 'The fixed distinctions suggested by it (the word unemployable) between "can work" and "can't work" or between "will work" and "won't work" are in reality fluid and indefinite'.

Clearly, since, except in Newcastle, spells of unemployment of very great length were very rare, the present research provides no evidence of groups of workers who are unemployable under any circumstances, or for that matter of groups who can be clearly identified as avoiding work under any circumstances. What it does show, on the other hand, is that in the depressed economic conditions of late 1971 and early 1972 the burden of unemployment fell

140

disproportionately upon certain groups, amongst whom the elderly, the unfit and low skilled were the most prominent.

The findings for Hammersmith suggested that the best way of reducing the burden of unemployment upon these specific groups is provided by securing a low overall unemployment rate. However, there are clearly ways of shifting the burden of unemployment, while not reducing its overall impact, which may be appropriate in the interests of some kind of social equity. In this respect, clearly, the elderly are the most difficult to help, while the disabled are the group who have been given the most attention by policy makers in the past. The position of the low skilled, however, as a group which has received very little attention in the past, merits special comment. This study probably, therefore, makes a special contribution in throwing light upon their difficulties in the labour market, since they have received less popular recognition than is the case with the other two disadvantaged groups.

It is a commonly held view that the unskilled have little reason to be unemployed, because they can respond to the vast generalised demand for non-specific types of labour which is never entirely absent. Department of Employment regulations safeguard skilled men from punitive action if they fail to take work below their skill levels, but of course unskilled men do not have a comparable protected position. Similarly, the Supplementary Benefits Commission recognises that 'the more skill and experience a man has had in his chosen occupation, the longer he should be allowed to seek such work before being urged to consider alternatives'. (*Supplementary Benefits Handbook*)

It is not intended here to argue against the safeguards provided for skilled men, but rather to suggest that comparable consideration is required for the rest of the labour force. In fact, there are several crucial points to be made about the employment position of the unskilled man. First, as was shown in Chapter 1, while there are always vacancies for the unskilled available, there is also a vast excess of unskilled unemployed men over vacancies. Second, it is wrong to regard the unskilled as an undifferentiated mass, for at very low levels of skill significant discriminations may be made by employers between men with or without specific kinds of past occupational or industrial experience. Furthermore, where no skill or experience is required at all, the employers will nevertheless be seeking the best bargain in terms of the maximum of strength or speed of work against the minimum of pay. Such an equation will, for example, put the athletic student of 18 seeking vacation work at a substantial advantage as compared with a semi-literate family man of 40. Similarly, where heavy work is not involved the possibility of the payment of lower wages to women may result in employers offering them work in place of men. Third, at times when skilled work is scarce the skilled man becomes a competitor for the unskilled man's job. All these factors suggest that it may be misleading to

141

assume that there is work for unskilled men, just because in that sector of the labour market there are always new jobs arising. While some individuals may be able to chop and change very easily between these unsatisfactory low skilled jobs, as seemed to be the case with many young men in Hammersmith, others, who cannot readily be distinguished from the mass without special attention to their circumstances, unless they stand out because of their age or ill health, may find it very difficult to secure unskilled jobs.

Reflections on Policies for the Unemployed

This study supports Beveridge's view that there is a need to see policies for the relief of unemployment in terms of two levels of need, a need to push up general employment levels and a need to try to ensure that certain individuals do not turn up again and again in the dole queues. It also recognises that the problem of unemployment is only one of a number of social problems, such as low pay and the low levels of provision of aid to other disadvantaged groups, which need to be seen in a general context of social inequality.

It is important to face up to the difficulty associated with some of the policy arguments that have been developed in relation to disadvantaged groups in a general situation of educational inequality. To take an example from the first of the specific measures to be discussed, undoubtedly many men in the samples would benefit from a great expansion and development of Government training schemes, but without accompanying policies to ensure very high levels of employment the result will be either (a) merely to push up the qualifications needed for the lowest skilled jobs, or (b) to produce the displacement of men who currently hold jobs to make way for the products of training centres.

In Sweden industrial training is very much more developed than in Britain, and is vastly expanded at times of recessions (see Mukherjee). It is regarded as a contra-cyclical measure, while at the same time a recession is seen as the ideal opportunity to raise the skills of the labour force. In this way the present recession in towns like Coventry could be seen as the opportunity to provide skills for the semi- and unskilled who are so predominant among the long-term unemployed there. Once the economy returns to its typical post-war level there employers will soon find skilled workers very scarce. Recently Thirlwell (*British Journal of Industrial Relations*, July 1972) has drawn attention to the tendency of the demand and supply of labour to be badly adjusted to each other as far as specific industries and specific skills are concerned when there is so called 'full employment'. Clearly training and re-training have important roles to play in relation to this problem.

The lack of specific skill is obviously linked for most workers with the lack of more than minimum education. In addition this study has drawn attention

142

to the fact that a not insignificant number of unemployed men acknowledged themselves to be almost illiterate. At the present time men are not accepted for industrial training if they lack the educational background to benefit from a course. This must exclude a significant number of the men whom this study has identified as suffering employment problems primarily because of their lack of skill. The Department of Employment, in the booklet issued in February 1972 to stimulate discussion on the future of industrial training (*Training for the Future – A Plan for Discussion*), refers to the possibility of including some measure of education as well as training in their future provisions. An additional advantage of such a development is that it would increase the possibilities of training for white collar work. In this respect it is encouraging to note that the education authorities are being more closely involved than hitherto in planning the future provision of industrial training courses. Again on this point there is a great deal to be learnt from Sweden, where most courses are provided by the Board of Education on behalf of the Labour Market Board, and where the authorities are deeply conscious of a need to extend contemporary education facilities to people who completed their schooling when their scope was much more restricted. There is a conflict in Sweden between those who see training as something to be limited to equipping men with skills just sufficient to get them work and those who have wider educational objectives, but in general there is a deeper consciousness of the importance of meeting the needs of the unemployed men themselves than there is in Britain. Further evidence of the way in which the British training scheme has been narrowly limited, except for the disabled, to meeting the immediate and explicit needs of employers is found in the fact that courses are not limited to the unemployed. In practice a high proportion of all those attending training centres were in employment just prior to going there. The tendency for this to be the case is reinforced by the fact that the waiting periods for courses are very long, so that in general it does not pay the unemployed to wait to attend them.

Many men in the samples had never heard of government training courses. This finding was similar to one of Wedderburn's about redundant workers, but it may be argued that it is rather more disturbing to find such a high level of ignorance about courses in a group of unemployed men, many of whom had been and were to remain out of work a long while, than amongst a group of redundant workers, most of whom became re-employed very quickly. Of course, while training course places are so few it is perhaps inevitable, as with other scarce resources in the social services, that only restricted efforts are made to acquaint men of their availability. The plans announced by the Department of Employment to increase their supply of G.T.C. places from 11,000 to 17,000 by 1975 are to be welcomed in this context. It is to be hoped that this will involve some further opening up of opportunities for the unemployed, and is

143

not merely part of a process of shifting the emphasis from training by employers to training by the Government. The booklet *Training for the Future* reports a waiting list of 10,000 people for the existing G.T.C. places. What is needed in the long run is not just a response to largely unstimulated demand but a positive campaign to get government training to individuals who know nothing about it or consider themselves unqualified for it.

A substantial proportion of the men in the sample who knew about government training said they were too old for it. There is no formal maximum age for consideration for training, but it will be only natural that cost benefit considerations come into play when men with relatively short working lives ahead of them apply for, or enquire about, government training. Furthermore this process of informal rejection will inevitably be reinforced by a tendency for elderly men to rule themselves out for training. It is striking, however, how marked is the difference, even in Newcastle, between the employment prospects of men over 40 who are registered for skilled work and those who are registered for semi- or unskilled work. Of course the older man will be rather far down the queue while there is a long waiting list for G.T.C. places, therefore a humane view of the plight of these men requires more places to ensure that those who were valued by the economy while they were young and fit can be trained so that employers will continue to need them.

Some people have suggested that one appropriate response to the heavy unemployment amongst elderly men may be to reduce the retirement age. Superficially this has a certain attractiveness, reducing the psychological pressure upon men who are often deeply sensitive to what they see as the stigma of unemployment. In this context the increasing tendency of both the Department of Employment and the Supplementary Benefits Commission to reduce the pressure on older unemployed men, to make it clear to them that no one regards their unemployment as their own fault, is to be welcomed.

Civil servants often retire at 60 and many middle class people regard early retirement as a blessing rather than a curse. However this is retirement on an above average income. By contrast a period of enforced retirement beginning in the early fifties, throughout which a man is sustained only by a social security income, may be the start of a period of poverty lasting twenty or thirty years. Savings for retirement may be depleted many years before the age of 65 is even reached. A comment was made earlier about the need to see sums of redundancy pay, which at the outset appear quite large, in this kind of context. For this reason, therefore, while it is acknowledged that in the present state of the economy many of the elderly men interviewed for this study, and particularly those living in Newcastle are, in fact, unlikely to work again, it is considered that the apparently humanitarian move entailed in giving formal recognition to the inevitable could in the long run, in the absence of radical changes in the
144

level of provision for the retired, have serious consequences for the extent of poverty amongst the old. In addition there are some important and awkward questions that need to be asked about the impact of such a development upon the sense of personal 'worth' of the individuals involved. If men do not want to retire, then to re-define men under 65 as retired for the purposes of official statistics would not really reduce unemployment in its true sense.

One way of assisting the elderly unemployed to get work which is deserving of further consideration is the adoption of some kind of quota system. Under such a system employers would be required to seek to achieve a certain proportion of workers over a defined age in their labour force. Such a policy would operate as a constraint on the sacking of older workers, and would assist elderly unemployed men to get back to work. It would be easier to enforce than the quota system for disabled workers because of the simplicity of an age criterion. Experiments along these lines are currently proceeding in Sweden; they should be studied with care to see if there is anything Britain can learn from them.

In Chapter 5 a brief report was included on the unemployed men's view of the employment service. It must be admitted (a) that it was a very partial and subjective picture of the situation, and (b) that it was a picture of the service at a time when vacancies were running at the lowest level since the war. In the comments that follow, therefore, there will be no attempt to criticise the actual job that the Employment Exchanges were doing in the difficult conditions of October 1971. Rather what will be discussed will be the attempt that is going on at present to alter the nature, and the image, of the employment service. This must be examined carefully in the light of what this study has revealed about the characteristics of those who suffer most from unemployment.

In December 1971 the Department of Employment published a short booklet *People and Jobs,* setting out its plans to modernise the employment service. Its main proposals were summarised as follows in the Department of Employment Gazette:

a new Management framework will be established so that the service becomes a self managing unit — a departmental agency — within the department;
work on employment and unemployment benefit to be separated administratively and physically;
facilities for 'self service' and vacancy display to be fully extended;
the job of employment staff giving interviews to be thoroughly analysed and revalued;
the Professional and Executive Register to be restyled and charges made to employers for the service;
a new division of responsibility between the service and local education authorities for guidance and placing advice for young people;

145

a new network of better employment offices, located, designed and presented to encourage employers and workers to use them, and based on areas corresponding to local labour markets;

experimental development of the role of employment offices in providing local labour market intelligence.

These proposals are, of course, to be welcomed, leading, as it is hoped they will, to the development of a network of offices which can stand comparison with private agencies in terms of both standards of services and standards of accommodation. Furthermore, it is encouraging to see that the Department of Employment has noted, as this survey confirms, that the professional and executive element of the unemployed are so small a group that the tendency for expenditure on services for them to become an increasing charge on the public purse in recent years is not entirely justified.

However, there is a disturbing element, as far as those most vulnerable to unemployment are concerned, in this move to modernise the employment service. In *People and Jobs* one of the main objectives of the reform was described as follows (p. 5):

The Employment service in its present form is not however, able to grasp the opportunities which undoubtedly exist in a modern labour market. The majority of workers who register with the employment office are those claiming unemployment benefit. For this reason the Service is regarded by many workers and employers as a service for the unemployed — and mainly for manual workers at that. As a result employers do not inform the Service of all their vacancies and some hardly use it at all. During the past five years for example workers registering for jobs have normally outnumbered notified vacancies by more than two to one. Thus, whereas the Service fills more than two in three vacancies it places only about one in three of those who register.

The task facing the Service is to break out of a situation where employers do not use it because they doubt — sometimes rightly — whether it has suitable people on its books, and where workers seeking jobs do not visit the local employment office because vacancies they want are not notified by the employer.

Without either compulsory notification of vacancies or control over the development of private employment agencies it is inevitable that a substantial sector of the labour market will operate fairly satisfactorily without intervention from the Employment Exchanges. It may be that the national economy will work better if the employment services can break into this sector rather more,

146

though there is little evidence for such a judgement. What seems more questionable, however, is the implication, apparent in the fact that it was found necessary to point out in *People and Jobs* that the Employment Service is seen as 'for the unemployed and mainly for manual workers at that', that the traditional clientele of the services are to be regarded as some kind of handicap to it. The Employment Exchanges were set up to assist the unemployed, and low skilled manual workers have always formed a major part of this group. They are moreover that part of the unemployed who most need help from some government agency. Whilst it is true that a substantial part of the placing work done by the Exchange is with unskilled workers, it is also true that the ratio of unemployed to vacancies is enormously unfavourable to the unskilled.

If, in order to pursue what a Department of Employment official has described as a 'hard nosed' policy, a policy of letting economic and accounting considerations override any others, it is necessary for the Exchanges to shift from a policy of primarily helping the unemployed to one of devoting much time to enabling men in work to shift from one employer to another, this change of priorities ought to be made quite explicit. It is interesting to note that when he set up the Employment Exchange system in 1909, Churchill declared that 'the object will be ... to deal with men who have been waiting longest, as far as possible, and relieve their needs with some regard to the general purpose of rotation' (Hansard, 16 June 1909). There is a fundamental value issue at stake here, which should be widely debated in Parliament and elsewhere and not merely set out in a comparatively obscure document announcing what appear to be welcome administrative changes. Furthermore, there are even economic grounds for questioning this change of emphasis. Thus Thirlwell has argued in a recent paper (p. 176):

it would appear that for the same average expenditure on placing the benefits to be derived from speeding up the re-employment of the unemployed are likely to surpass the benefits from speeding up redeployment ...
There is almost certainly considerable underspending, in relation to potential benefits, on services to re-employ the unemployed, particularly in certain parts of the country where the probability of remaining on the unemployment register for any given length of time is higher than the average for the nation.

People and Jobs talks vaguely about the development of special services to help the hard to place; it is important that these are not lost sight of in the general eagerness to get away from the 'dole-queue image'. Yet current developments suggest that there is a severe danger that this will happen. Already the

Supplementary Benefits Commission has developed its own team of Unemployment Review Officers (U.R.Os) to give attention to unemployed men who remain in receipt of supplementary benefits for substantial periods of time. Whenever groups of these officials are brought together a great deal of talk can be heard about the way in which they are building up their own employment service by collecting information on vacancies and making contacts with employers. There are a number of reasons why it must be questioned whether it is a good thing that this ' second line' employment service should grow up, while the 'first line' service becomes increasingly uninterested in the problems of the long-term unemployed.

First, the Employment Exchanges have a great deal of experience. They have done, and are still doing, a great deal of work to build up contacts with employers all over the country. They possess a great deal of sophisticated information on the workings of national and local labour markets. For the Supplementary Benefits' staff to build up comparable expertise will involve excessive expenditures in time and money.

Second, there are some important points to be raised about the process by which a man moves from a situation in which his employment problems are primarily the concern of a Department of Employment officer, to one in which almost the only official attention he receives is from a U.R.O. In Chapter 4 it was shown that many of the unemployed were not receiving supplementary benefits, and that the major group getting this sort of benefit were those who had lost their entitlement to unemployment benefit on account of long unemployment in the current or previous spells of unemployment. So the great majority of men who come to the attention of the U.R.Os do so only after considerable unemployment, during which the Employment Exchange officials will have come to regard them as 'very poor placing prospects', if not entirely unemployable. Yet the U.R.O. is expected to start trying, with low resources compared with the Exchange staff, to help men who will be demoralised themselves, and perhaps stigmatised by employers, because of their already long unemployment.

Third, there is a coercive aspect to the whole situation. Men who reach the attention of the U.R.Os are 'expected' — to a greater or lesser degree — to get work. Indeed they may be warned of the possibility of prosecution for their failure to maintain themselves and their dependents, or harrassed in other more 'informal' ways. It is recognised that progress is being made towards the development of a more sensitive and supportive role for U.R.Os (see Stevenson, Chapters 4 and 5), but it is nevertheless invidious that men who have been regarded as virtually unemployable by the Department of State responsible for helping the unemployed to find work should then come to the attention of another department, which will have different expectations of them.

148

Finally, there is an element of stigma in the parallel development of employment services. The British employment service developed out of a recognition that unemployment was an economic problem, a problem that could not be left to the Poor Law, with its conception of worklessness as a consequence of idleness and sloth. But today there is a danger that a distinction will be made between those whose unemployment is just a temporary problem of movement from one job to another, and those whose unemployment results from a seriously disadvantaged position in the labour market, in such a way that the latter becomes the prime concern of the organisation which has taken over the legacy of the Poor Law, while the former get the benefit of all the modern developments in methods of counselling, placing and training for employment.

Seen as a measure to segregate tasks and increase specialisation, or to increase the flow of resources to the employment service, the hiving off of benefit payment is wholly desirable. But is the implication that this is a source of 'stigma', because of the traditional way in which it was administered or because of its clientele? If it is merely the former then the main remedies lie in the further development of techniques to get away from the dole queue, registration by post or even by telephone for example, and to treat the recipients of social security benefits as people who have every right to expect a first class service. If it is the latter, on the other hand, then such a reform, however desirable it may be in other ways, will have serious consequences for the men who have been the subject of this study.

The low take-up of Supplementary Benefits by men in this study, leaving men with incomes below the official 'poverty level', could be said to provide some evidence that a stigma attached to this form of benefit is still felt. However, it was also shown that a remarkably large proportion of the men had no clear idea of the kinds of benefits they were getting, so perhaps more important than stigma in keeping down the number of applications for supplementary benefits is simple ignorance of what is available. In as much as this is the case, the proposal to separate the payment of unemployment benefit from the employment service would have the most beneficial effect if it led to the integration of the administration and payment of benefits for unemployed men with those for all other kinds of social security benefits. The Department of Health and Social Security are gradually developing 'integrated' offices to enable the payment of supplementary benefits and of pensions and sickness benefits to be co-ordinated better. It would be very advantageous for their clients if all kinds of benefits for the unemployed could be administered from these offices too.

At the same time, the demonstration in this study that very many men are quite confused about the difference between unemployment benefit, supplementary benefit and earnings-related supplement should raise the question

149

whether the distinction between insurance benefits and other kinds of relief which governments have struggled to maintain since the First World War is really necessary, or whether a much more totally integrated system of support for the unemployed should not be devised. The association of this distinction with very muddled notions of stigma is well discussed in Olive Stevenson's book on Supplementary Benefits (see particularly pp. 18, 19).

A reference was made earlier to the rather general statements in *People and Jobs* about services for the hard to place. The Department of Employment has been engaged on a review of its services for the disabled and an examination of the problems of people they define as 'socially handicapped'.

At present the Department of Employment has a number of ways of helping the disabled. It runs a special service organised by Disablement Resettlement Officers, which seeks to place disabled men in work by giving special attention to their problems and building up good contacts with employers. In this object it is aided by the quota system, described on p. 133, which is of primary value as a means of securing voluntary compliance with the aim of getting disabled people to work, rather than as something to be enforced by coercive measures.

There are also special rehabilitation and training courses for the disabled, a limited number of 'sheltered' factories, and two occupations (car park and lift attendants) reserved for the disabled.

The main weakness of the 'traditional' service for the disabled is that its success depends very much on the willing co-operation of employers. This problem has been exacerbated latterly as the categories of the disabled which the Disablement Resettlement Service has to deal with have changed a little from the unambiguously physically disabled, often the casualties of the two wars, to increasing numbers of men with mental illnesses of various kinds. The service not only finds it more difficult to help this new kind of clientele, but it also finds it very difficult to achieve a clear definition of who should be its concern, and particularly who should be 'registered' as disabled.

This situation, together with some of the 'placing problems' faced by its non-specialist employment officers, has led to a desire to single out a new category of people who need help, 'people with distinct social or personal problems – the "socially handicapped" ' (*People and Jobs*, p. 18). These are seen as 'an as yet ill-defined group of people whose problems in getting or holding down satisfactory jobs are often part of wider domestic and social difficulties'. (*Ibid*).

These so-called 'socially handicapped' people will be very much more the concern of the second report on this research. However, the experience so far with the methodological and theoretical problems entailed in identifying special problem groups by the use of broad statistical techniques suggests that the Department of Employment will find it very difficult to develop broad 'rules

150

of thumb' for identifying the socially handicapped. Are they going to single out the elderly unskilled in Newcastle, or the elderly single in Hammersmith, for the attention of a special service? Or do they want to develop more sophisticated filters than these? If the latter is the case then surely there will be a need for an elaborate screening process, that will make it necessary for them to maintain a thorough service for all the unemployed. The 'socially handicapped' will only emerge as people in need of special help as their spell of unemployment lengthens. Then, if a Department of Employment service for the 'socially handicapped' is developed, are situations going to be allowed to occur in which after doing a certain amount of work with unemployed men the Department of Employment specialist officers pass those with the most severe problems on to the U.R.Os of the Supplementary Benefits Commission? Or situations in which two types of specialist help are given by different departments at the same time? There are some important issues here, to which the second report on this project will return. All that can be said here is that if readers are sceptical about some of the attempts of this survey to identify 'problem groups', and particularly about the finding that the criterion of disablement which correlates most successfully with unemployment length is a subjective one, they should be equally dubious about any plans that may be developed to screen out the 'socially handicapped'.

Swedish vocational rehabilitation officials, who recognise a category of 'socially handicapped' people amongst the individuals who they help, are quite ready to acknowledge that the people they describe thus are individuals whose disabilities they cannot classify under any more specific heading. A prominent group amongst their 'socially handicapped' are ex-prisoners and others with criminal records, but they also classify people under this heading whose only handicap is that they live far from job vacancies and are reluctant to move. Very many of the low skilled, low income unemployed have some 'social problem' to cope with. The experience of this survey suggests that the label 'socially handicapped' will tend to be applied to those who remain out of work a long while and whose difficulties cannot be explained in any other way. Is it not better to recognise that these are a group who should be the main concern of the employment service, rather than to give them a special name and pass them on to a special section? There is a danger that people who get classified as a peripheral problem group in this way end up getting the worst service, and not the best.

The best way to ensure that the elderly get work, that employers take on their full quota of disabled workers, that the 'socially handicapped' do not become a major 'problem' group for the employment service, and so on, is to ensure that the unemployment rate is kept to its lowest possible level. Furthermore, it is only against a background of a resolve to maintain really full employment that special services for the most disadvantaged groups can achieve real successes and avoid a situation in which each man who is helped into work is not replaced by another 'social casualty' who is thrown out of work. How 'full' really full employment should be entails a political question which must be tackled, not by taking economists' definitions of it for granted, but by seeking economic solutions in a context in which concern for the need to minimise the impact of unemployment is treated as of prime importance.

Methodological appendix

The major part of the data was collected by means of a survey conducted with a random sample of men drawn from the live register at the Employment Exchanges within the three areas on 1 October 1971. However, in order to draw on background material from the census and local authorities, only men who lived within local authority boundaries were included. The sampling fractions used were one in ten in Coventry and Newcastle and one in five in Hammersmith. The total sample sizes that resulted were Coventry 500, Hammersmith 395, and Newcastle 544. From these samples the following response rates were achieved: Coventry 372 interviews i.e. 74%, Hammersmith 232 interviews i.e. 74% and Newcastle 414 interviews i.e. 76%.

The non-response, which was predominantly a matter of non-contact rather than refusals, came mainly from two groups of men. Firstly, some of the men had returned to work. These were much more difficult to contact as they could only be interviewed in the evening. Even though interviewers were instructed to make a special effort with this group of men, most of them disliked evening interviews and thus this group did not receive the degree of perseverance from the interviewing team that we would have liked. The further problem encountered with this group was that when contacted many indicated a reluctance to be interviewed; because they were back at work they did not think that they were relevant to the survey, and were not particularly keen to be reminded of their recent unemployment. Secondly, there was the group of men who were transients, only staying one or two nights in the local hostels or lodging houses. If these men were not interviewed within the first few days of the survey, they were often difficult to trace. This group were a particular problem in Hammersmith, which probably accounts for the very slightly lower response rate in that area.

Statistical information gathered by the Department of Employment for the pilot survey indicated that the non-respondents were fairly evenly distributed in terms of age, skill and marital status. It was not possible, because of the considerable work involved, to obtain this information for the main samples.

The questionnaire, which is reproduced at the end of this appendix, was administered by interviewers carefully chosen, trained, and supervised by a member of the main research team stationed in each area for the duration of the study. While interviewers had a very wide range of qualifications, they were generally chosen from people with past experience of social survey work.

Because of the nature of the survey and also the many topics of a highly personal nature in the questionnaire, a high degree of care was taken in the selection of interviewers. This, the authors believe, is one of the main reasons for a fairly good response rate. Because of a fairly high percentage of Asian immigrants in the Coventry area, an interviewer fluent in Urdu, Hindi and Punjabi was employed the response rate from this group was extremely high.

In addition to the material collected from the survey, information on the men interviewed was also obtained from official records in the Department of Employment and the Department of Health and Social Security. This information covered the mens' work and health records for the last three years, occupations registered at the employment exchange, benefit positions at the time the sample was drawn, which included whether or not they were in receipt of supplementary benefit or earnings related supplement to unemployment benefit.

Apart from giving important and accurate information, the knowledge gained from the mens' records gave the opportunity to check the material collected by the interviewers. In no cases were any major discrepancies discovered.

As well as the information gathered from the above-mentioned government departments, the Home Office supplied information on criminal records of men in the samples where applicable. This permission was granted with very strict conditions of security and confidentiality, which will be discussed further at the end of this appendix.

In order that the longer term unemployed would not be under-represented, it was decided that there should be a six months follow up period after the date on which the sample was drawn. This was necessary in order that those who were just about to commence on a longish period of unemployment at the time the sample was drawn were not omitted. The follow up was carried out by inserting a card in the claim documents kept by the Employment Exchanges for all the men chosen for the sample. These cards were returned to the research headquarters when the men ceased to register as unemployed. When the six months was up a search was made of all the claims from which cards had not been returned. If the cards had gone astray the Exchange informed us of the date at which registration ceased, otherwise the men were counted as unemployed for the full six month period.

The measures taken to safeguard confidentiality should be mentioned. The authors wish to state most emphatically the high degree of importance that they attached to this matter. This was especially so with the nature and amount of material made available for us. It should also be mentioned that this very high regard for confidentiality was also felt by all those civil servants who supplied information for the study.

Everyone employed in the research was required to sign the Official Secrets Act. These included the interviewers and those employed to assist the work of

154

gathering information from the government departments. After selection for the sample all the men were sent a letter from the Parliamentary Under Secretary of State for the Department of Health and Social Security. The letter requested that an interview be granted to a member of the research team, and stated that if an interview were granted it would be understood that this also signified the granting of permission for the research team to see his records. It was also stated that any information given to the interviewer would not be made known to any government department in any way that would enable the man to be identified personally. The latter condition was most rigidly applied. No member of any government department was allowed to see a completed interview schedule. The information was collected by a member of the research team with a clerical assistant from outside the government departments concerned.

Interviewers were instructed to call at the address of a man drawn in the sample up to six times. They were expected to make some reasonable attempts to persuade hesitant individuals to co-operate; however a firm refusal was to be treated as such, and the man bothered no further. Only one man took the trouble of writing to the Under Secretary of State asking that an interviewer not call.

Criminal records were supplied on the condition that they were not shown to anyone outside the research team, and that they were kept under lock and key and destroyed when the appropriate information had been extracted.

In connection with as many as possible of the findings reported in Chapters 3, 4 and 5, chi square tests of statistical significance have been carried out to try to ascertain whether the associations discovered are sufficiently strong to have been unlikely to have arisen as a result of chance peculiarities in the samples chosen. Wherever findings are reported as statistically significant this means that the chi square test revealed that they would have been unlikely to have arisen by chance more than 5 times in a 100 ($p = < .05$). On many occasions better 'significance' levels than this are reported, as $p = < .02$ (twice in a 100) or $p = < .01$ (once in a 100). The levels are sometimes quoted as the 5, 2 and 1 per cent levels. The statistical safeguards relevant to the A.I.D. analysis reported in Chapter 6 are described in the text.

UNIVERSITY OF OXFORD UNEMPLOYMENT SURVEY

1(a)   Are you still registered as unemployed?

                                                Yes
                                                No
                                                D.K.
                                                NA/Refusal

1(b)   *(If no) Are you*

                        Back in full time work on a permanent basis?
                        Back in full time work on a temporary basis?
                        Doing part-time work?
                        Sick?
                        Retired?
                        Unemployed but not registering?
                        Another reply
                        (Specify...
                        ....)
                        D.K.
                        N.A./Refusal

1(c)   *(If working full-time)*

                        What date did you return to work?
                       1971

1(d)   *(If working full-time)*

                        What kind of work are you doing?
                Occupation

        Industry

2   Where were you born?

                        Town and district

                        County

3   How old are you? *(Write in number of years)*

156

4   Are you

Married?
Single?
Divorced?
Separated?
Widowed?
Any other answers
(Specify..
....
D.K.
Refusal

5   *Before completing details of the household interviewers should establish whether:-*

Respondent is living in (i) a private dwelling
(ii) a commercial establishment or other institution
D.K.
Refusal

If response (2) is given to question 5 go to question 8

DETAILS OF HOUSEHOLD

6   Can you tell me who else, if anyone, lives in your household? I mean by 'household' people who live here regularly and are catered for by the same person as yourself. Would you say also if you board or lodge here? *(In this instance interviewers should insert B or L after the respondent)*

Member of household (write in relationship to respondent)	Sex (M or F)	Age	Employment position (if over 15)
1 Respondent			
2			
3			
4			
5			
6			
7			
8			
9			
10			

157

7   Who is the Head of Household? That is, the person who is responsible for rent or who owns the house. *(Interviewers should ring the appropriate number under Question 6)*

8(a)   Have you any commitment to support any family member or relatives who are not living with you at present?

Yes
No
D.K.
Refusal

8(b)   *(If yes to 8(a))*
Is this commitment to any of the following

Wife and children?
Wife?
Children?
Parent/Parents?
Anyone else/or any combination not listed above? (Specify...........

....

D.K.
N/A/Refusal

8(c)   *(If commitment to wife and/or children)*
Is this a voluntary commitment or one that has been imposed by the courts?

Voluntary
Court order
D.K.
NA/Refusal

8(d)   *(If reply to 8(c) 'a court order')*

How much do you have to pay each week? *(Write in amount in two figures to the nearest pound, putting 98 for D.K., and 99 for NA/Refusal)*

158

DETAILS OF ACCOMMODATION OCCUPIED

9 Respondents household is living in:

    (a) Whole house
    (b) Purpose-built flat or maisonette
    (c) Converted flat
    (d) Other self-contained accommodation (e.g.
       caravan or houseboat)
    (e) Rooms
    (f) As lodger } In one of the
    (g) or boarder } above
    (h) Hostel/Lodging house
    (i) Boarding house/Hotel
    (j) Other institution
    (k) Anywhere else (Specify.............................)
    (l) D.K.
    (m) Refusal

Questions 10 to 15 should only be asked of private households occupying the first five categories of accommodation specified in question 9.

10 How many rooms does your household have for its own use, that is that are not shared with other households?
(A room includes kitchens but does not include bathroom, w.c., hall etc. Write in total number, coding 7+ as 7, D.K. as 8 and refusals as 9).

11 Does your household have the use of a fixed bath/shower?

       Sole use
       Shared use (with other households)
       None
       D.K.
       NA/Refusal

12 Does your household have the use of a cold water tap?

       Sole use
       Shared use
       None
       D.K.
       NA/Refusal

13   Does your household have the use of a hot water tap?

> Sole use
> Shared use
> None
> D.K.
> NA/Refusal

14   Does your household have the use of a w.c.?

> Inside — sole use
> Inside — shared use
> Outside — sole use
> Outside — shared use
> None
> D.K.
> NA/Refusal

Spece for calculating total number of housing deprivations

15   Do you (does the head of the household) own or rent this accommodation?

> Owns/is buying
> Rents from Local Authority
> Rents privately — unfurnished
> Rents privately — furnished
> Service tenancy
> Local authorities homeless families accommodation
> Other (Specify....................................
> ....
> D.K.
> NA/Refusal

16   *(ASK ALL)*   How much do you pay in rent/mortgage/board and lodgings/for your keep? *(Substitute the appropriate term. Ask about rates if paid, and work out from all the information you are given a weekly figure in pounds and pence, to four figures, to insert in the coding box. If in doubt how to proceed collect all the necessary figures and consult your supervisor. Do not include sums paid for additional amenities such as heating or garages if these are known. Code 'D.K.' 9998 and 'Refusal' 9999).*

Now I have some questions on your health

17   Do you have any condition which you or others might consider a physical or mental disability?

Yes
No
D.K.
NA/Refusal

If 'yes' to Q. 17 ask questions 18–23 inclusive. Otherwise proceed to 1. 24

18   What is that disability? *(Specify fully, bearing in mind that there may be more than one disability)*

19   Are you having treatment for your disability (ies) from a doctor or hospital?

Yes
No
D.K.
NA/Refusal

20   Are you registered at the Employment Exchange as a disabled person?

Yes
Application under consideration
No
D.K.
NA/Refusal

21(a)   *(If 'no' to q. 20)* Have you applied for registration?

Yes
No
D.K.
NA/Refusal

21(b)   *(If 'yes' to q. 21(a))* Why was this unsuccessful?

21(c)   *(If 'no' to q. 21(a))* Why is this?

22(a)   As a result of your disability have you had to change your occupation?

> Yes
> No
> D.K.
> NA/Refusal

22(b)   *(If 'yes' to q. 22(a))*

What are the most significant changes you have had to make? *(Do not prompt. Code up to three changes)*

(a)	Change in work environment
(b)	Change to less responsible work
(c)	Change from non-manual to manual
(d)	Change from manual to non-manual
(e)	Change to less skilled work
(f)	Change in conditions of employment (hours, shifts etc.)
(g)	Change to less well paid work
(h)	Prepared to stop looking for work
(i)	Others (Specify..
	....
(j)	D.K.
(k)	NA/Refusal

23(a)   Does your disability limit your chances of getting work?

> Yes
> No
> D.K.
> NA/Refusal

23(b)   *If yes to q. 23(a)*

How are your chances limited? *(Do not prompt. Code up to three ways)*

(a)	Can only do light work
(b)	Can only do sheltered work
(c)	Employers discriminate
(d)	Employees discriminate
(e)	Can only work limited number of hours
(f)	Can only work at home
(g)	Unable to use public transport
(h)	Others − specify
(i)	D.K.
(j)	NA/Refusal

162

24(a)   Are you at present having treatment from a doctor or hospital for
        any (other) complaint(s)?

                              Yes
                              No
                              D.K.
                              NA/Refusal

If yes to q. 24(a)

24(b)   What is your complaint?
        *(If more than one complaint ask what he considers his most serious
        complaint)*

25   Is there any other way (not so far mentioned) in which your health
        affects your work?

                        No
                        Yes effects of injury
                        Recurrent Illness
                        Other — specify
                        D.K.
                        NA

26   Do you consider yourself fit for work now?

                                  Yes
                                  No
                                  D.K.
                                  NA/Refusal

27(a)   Have you ever lost a job because you were unable to perform your
        work due to the effects of alcohol?

                              Yes
                              No
                              D.K.
                              NA/Refusal

27(b)   *(If 'yes' to q. 27(a))* When did this last happen?

                        Date...

27(c)   *(If 'yes' to q. 27(a))* How many times has this happened? *(Write in number treating 7 or more as 7, and only using 8 if any man says don't know, and 9 if he refuses to answer or the question is inapplicable)*

28   Have you ever received treatment for a drinking problem?

                                                           Yes
                                                           No
                                                           D.K.
                                                           NA/Refusal

INCOME WHILE UNEMPLOYED

29   Were you in receipt of unemployment benefit in the week ending 1 October?

                     Yes
                     No
                     D.K.
                     Refusal

30(a)   Were you in receipt of earnings related supplement to unemployment benefit in the week ending 1 October?

                                        Yes
                                        No
                                        D.K.
                                        Refusal

30(b)   Were you in receipt of supplementary benefit in the week ending 1 October?

                     Yes
                     No
                     D.K.
                     Refusal

31   Were you and your wife (if applicable) in receipt of any of the following kinds of income in the week ending 1 October?

                     (a)   Family Allowances   Yes
                                                  No
                                                  D.K.
                                                  Refusal

    (If 'yes') How much did you receive?   ....

(b)   War Pension

                              Yes
                              No
                              D.K.
                              Refusal

(If 'yes') How much did you receive?   ....

(c)   Industrial Injury/Disablement Pension

                              Yes
                              No
                              D.K.
                              Refusal

(If 'yes') How much did you receive?   ....

(d)   Family Income Supplement

                              Yes
                              No
                              D.K.
                              Refusal

(If 'yes') How much did you receive?   ....

(e)   Occupational Pension

                              Yes
                              No
                              D.K.
                              Refusal

(If 'yes') How much did you receive?   ....

31 *cont.*

(f)   Payments from lodgers, boarders and tenants

                              Yes
                              No
                              D.K.
                              Refusal

(If 'yes') How much did you receive?   ....

     (g)   Own earnings

                    Yes
                    No
                    D.K.
                    Refusal

(If 'yes') How much did you receive?   ....

     (h)   Wife's earnings

                    Yes
                    No
                    D.K.
                    Refusal

(If 'yes') How much did she receive?   ....

     (i)   Other Income (apart from unemployment
         and supplementary benefits)

                    Yes
                    No
                    D.K.
                    Refusal

(If 'yes') How much did you receive?   ....

Write in total amount received from all the above sources (to nearest £, two figures)

EDUCATION

32   I would like to ask you a few questions about your education; firstly,
How old were you when you left school?

                    15 and below
                    16
                    17
                    18
                    D.K.
                    Refusal

33   What kind of school was the last one you attended?

No schooling at all
Elementary/Secondary Modern
State Grammar/Central/Technical
Comprehensive/Bilateral
Direct Grant/Private/Public School
Other British
All foreign schools, including Eire
D.K.
Refusal

34   Did you have any qualifications when you left school?
*(General principle where more than one kind of qualification held
code highest one in this list. But see interviewers' handbook for
detailed instructions.*

GCE 'A' Level, Higher and Scottish Higher
   School Certificate
GCE 'O' level, Matriculation, School Certificate,
   Scottish Certificate of Education
RSA/CSE/City and Guilds
Others (Specify..
....)
None
D.K.
Refusal

35(a)   Was your schooling in any way interrupted?

Yes
No
D.K.
NA/Refusal

(If yes to q. 35(a))
35(b)   For how long was it interrupted?

Up to one year
1 to 2 years
2 to 3 years
3+
D.K.
NA/refusal

167

35(c)   Why was your schooling interrupted?

Health
War
Family reasons
Others
D.K.
NA/Refusal

36(a)   Did you pursue any further education after leaving school?

Yes
No
D.K.
NA/Refusal

(If yes to q. 36(a) ask 36(b))

36(b)   Did you complete your course of study?

Yes
No
D.K.
NA/Refusal

36(c)   *If 'yes to q. 36(b) ask –* What qualification(s) did you obtain?
*(Note if more than one qualification stated code highest on list –
see also instruction in interviewer's handbook)*

(i)   No qualifications obtained
(ii)   University degree, higher degree (including
         medical training)
(iii)   Higher National Certificate or Diploma
(iv)   Teachers Certificate, Membership of a
         professional institution, full or inter-
         mediate professional qualifications,
         SRN
(v)   GCE 'A' Higher School Certificate,
         Intermediate Arts/Science
(vi)   Ordinary National Certificate or Diploma
(vii)   GCE 'O' level, Matriculation, General
         School Certificate
(viii)   City and Guilds, R.S.A., Forces Educational
         Certificates/Diplomas
(ix)   Others – specify...................................
(x)   D.K.
(xi)   NA/Refusal

168

37   Did you have any special schooling, at any of these kinds of schools
(Use prompt card or read list)

> No special schooling
> School for physically handicapped
> School for the deaf
> School for the blind
> School for backward children
> Approved school
> School for children with special talents
> e.g. art, music etc.
> Others (Specify..............................
> ....)
> D.K.
> Refusal

38   How well are you able to read and write in English?

> Well
> Not very well
> Not at all
> D.K.
> Refusal

WORK AND SKILL

Introduction I would like to ask you some questions about the kind
of work you do, and the kind of work you might like to do, together
with some questions about your period of unemployment. Firstly,
we would like to know:-

SKILL

39   What kind of work do you consider your usual occupation?
*(Interviewers please ensure, as will all questions about jobs, that you
obtain sufficient information to enable classification. Do not accept
answers like 'factory work'. If such answers are given ask the man to
describe the actual kind of work he did. Please note if he has never
worked)*

Job

169

40(a)   When you started this kind of work did it involve any period of training or learning the job?

(i)   No training
(ii)   Apprenticeship (Civilian or Army)
(iii)   Traineeship
(iv)   Government training (Specify...............
....
(v)   Armed service training (Refers only to training for what is also a civilian occupation)
(vi)   Professional training
(vii)   Other training (specify..........................
....
(viii) D.K.
(ix)   Refusal/NA

(If training undergone, ask 40(b))

40(b)   Did you complete this training?

Yes
No
D.K.
NA/Refusal

41(a)   Apart from the job you mentioned as your usual occupation are there any other kinds of work you have done?
(This refers to different kinds of work, not employers. If man says 'no' do not write anything. If he says 'don't know' or refuses to answer, note this. If he says 'yes' ask q. 41(b))

41(b)   What are these kinds of work, and what type of training did you receive, if any?

OCCUPATION	TRAINING *(insert code nos. used for 40(a))*
1.	
2.	
3.	
4.	
5.	
6.	

Total number of different kinds of work (taking q. 39 and 41(b) into account — maximum 7)

Total number of different kinds of training (40(a) plus 41(b)) Code 'O' for no training

WORK PATTERN VERSITILITY

42(a)   What was your last job? *(If man is now back at work, this refers to his job before the spell of unemployment)*

Job

Industry

(If last job was not in usual occupation — see q. 39 for this — ask q. 42(b))

42(b)   How long is it since you were employed in your usual occupation? *(Interviewers write in total number of months in coding column).*

43   Looking back on your working life, which of the following statements most accurately describes yours? *(Respondents to be given a prompt card)*

    (a)   All of your working life has been spent in the same occupation (irrespective of different employers)

    (b)   Not all your working life has been spent in *one* occupation, but you have done one particular kind of work longer than another.

    (c)   Although you have had a number of different occupations during your working life there has been one that you have done more often than others

    (d)   That you have worked in lots of different occupations, and that you don't think of yourself as having one occupation in particular

    (e)   That you have never worked

    (f)   D.K. Don't understand question

    (g)   Refusal

44   You have stated that your last job was...
      Could you also say what was your *(where same as one mentioned
      already write in 'same as first etc. Use D.K.' or 'none' where applicable)*
                        (a)   First job?
                               Industry

                        (b)   Best job?
                               Industry

                        (c)   Longest job?
                               Industry

45   How long did your longest job last?
      *(Interviewers write in amount to nearest year. Use 98 for D.K.,
      99 for NA/Refusal)*

46   *(Interviewers ask the following question for every different job given
      in the range of last, first, best, and longest. Where answer was 'same
      as last' etc. code 'not applicable').*
      Could you say why your............................job ended?

(a)	Made redundant, term of engagement completed @
(b)	Dismissed, where no other reason applies
(c)	Health reasons
(d)	Domestic reasons
(e)	Left to better self
(f)	Left voluntarily (job unsatisfactory)*
(g)	Left voluntarily (no reason given)+
(h)	Left or dismissed as a result of an offence against the law
(i)	Seasonal termination of job
(j)	Conscription
(k)	Other reasons (Specify..
(l)	No reason given/D.K.
(m)	Not applicable/Refusal

      @ Made redundant includes answers like job finished, and normal
        retirement. If man says he was made redundant voluntarily,
        his reason for doing this should be sought.
      * Job unsatisfactory includes complaints about pay, promotion,
        prospects, hours, security etc., if man did not have a better
        job to go to straight away, in which case 'left to better self'
        will apply.
      + Refers to such answers as 'chucked the job in because fed up',
        'felt like a change'.

47(a)   How old were you when you first became unemployed?
(Interviewers write in age in years)
(Use 98 for D.K., 99 for refusal)

47(b)   What year was that? *(Write in last two figures of year) (Use 98 for D.K., 99 for refusal)*

48   Could you say how many times you remember being unemployed? *(Interviewers write in the number in two figures – do not worry about achieving a high degree of accuracy if the number is large, e.g. approaching 20 or more. Use 98 for D.K., 99 for refusal)*

49   Could you say if any of the following restricts your prospects of getting a job?
(prompt, and code up to 3 in order of importance)

		(57–58/2) First mentioned	(59–60/2) Second mentioned	(61–62/2) Third mentioned
(a)	Physical health and disability	1	1	1
(b)	Recurrent illness	2	2	2
(c)	Domestic problems	3	3	3
(d)	Age	4	4	4
(e)	Psychological or emotional problems	5	5	5
(f)	Criminal record	6	6	6
(g)	None/N.A./Refusal	9	9	9

50(a)   Do you consider in recent years you have had difficulties in obtaining jobs?
        Yes
        No
        D.K.
        NA/Refusal

50(b)   Do you consider in recent years you have had difficulties in holding down jobs?
        Yes
        No
        D.K.
        NA/Refusal

50(c) *(If 'yes' to either 50(a) or (b) ask 50(c))*
Could you say what are the main reasons for your difficulties?
(Code up to 2 reasons)

(a)	Health/Disability
(b)	Economic factors
(c)	Seasonal factors
(d)	No jobs available at sufficient pay
(e)	No jobs available at my skill level
(f)	Domestic problems
(g)	Age
(h)	Bad work record
(i)	Criminal record
(j)	Little or no demand for skills
(k)	Racial discrimination
(l)	Others (Specify............................ ....
(m)	D.K.
(n)	NA/Refusal

51(a)   Are you looking for work?

Yes
No
D.K.
Refusal

(If 'yes' proceed to q. 52, if 'no' ask q. 51(b))

51(b)   Why are you not looking for work?
(code up to 2 reasons)

Back at work already
Awaiting recall to previous job
Believes no possibility of suitable job
Better off out of work
Commitments to family and/or relatives
Considers himself retired
Too old and/or too ill
Other reasons (Specify........................... ....
D.K.
NA/Refusal

*(Do not ask questions 52–57 of those who are not looking for work,
but ask 51(c) of any who replied 'back at work already' to q. 51(b))*

51(c)   How did you get your new job?

Through the employment exchange
By writing to ask if there were vacancies
By telephoning to ask if there were vacancies
By calling to ask if there were vacancies
Through a contact with a former workmate
Through a local paper
Through a national paper
By looking in a trade paper
By asking a friend or relative
Through a private employment agency
Through a trade union
It was found by a welfare organisation, probation
officer or social worker
D.K.
NA/Refusal

*(Answers 02, 03 and 04 only apply if man made contact without
knowing of any vacancies – it is the source of information which
concerns us)*

SELECTIVITY

52   Some people think it very important to get the right kind of work,
others don't really mind what they do. Apart from restrictions you
may have already mentioned would you say of yourself that you are:
(Prompt)

Extremely selective?
Fairly selective?
Not very selective?
None of these? (Specify.......
....)
D.K.
NA/Refusal

53(a)   Has anyone at the Employment Exchange or Ministry of Social
        Security, or a friend or relative ever said that you are too selective
        about the kind of work you will do?

                                        Yes
                                        No
                                        D.K.
                                        NA/Refusal

53(b)   *(If 'yes' to q. 53(a))* Who has said this to you?

                                        Employment Exchange
                                        Social Security
                                        Friend or relative
                                        Both Exchange and Social Security
                                        Other multiple answers
                                        (Specify......................................
                                        ....)
                                        D.K.
                                        NA/Refusal

54   Could you say what kinds of work you are prepared to consider at
        present?
                                        Same as usual occupation only
                                        Only job other than usual occupation
                                        Both usual and other jobs
                                        D.K.
                                        NA/Refusal

55(a)   Since you became unemployed have you changed your mind about
        the kind of work you are prepared to consider?
                                        Yes
                                        No
                                        D.K.
                                        NA/Refusal

55(b)   *(If 'yes' to q. 55(a)* Could you state the most important ways in which
        you have changed your mind? *(List up to 3 ways, for post coding).*

56   Have you tuned down any jobs offered during this spell of unemploy-
        ment? *(Interviewers write in number, treat 7+ as 7, D.K. as 8 and
        refusal/NA as 9)*

176

57   Could you say which of the following job seeking methods you have used during your current spell of unemployment and which have resulted in your finding a vacancy for which you have been interviewed? *(Interviewers note that where the method entails presentation in person e.g. factory gate, that interview means a discussion about an actual vacancy for which he is suitable with a suitable person, e.g. personnel manager or foreman, about taking a job for which the respondent is a suitable candidate and the interview concerns an actual vacancy).*

    (a)   Using Employment Exchange Services
                  Interview resulted
                  Used but no interview
                  Not used/D.K./N.A.

    (b)   Writing to firms to ask *if* they have any vacancies
                  Interview resulted
                  Used but no interview
                  Not used/DK/NA

    (c)   Calling at firms to ask if they have any vacancies
                  Interview resulted
                  Used but no interview
                  Not used/DK/NA

    (d)   Telephoning firms to ask if they have any vacancies
                  Interview resulted
                  Used but no interview
                  Not used/DK/NA

    (e)   Contacts with former workmates
                  Interview resulted
                  Used but no interview
                  Not used/DK/NA

    (f)   Looking in local newspapers
                  Interview resulted
                  Used but no interview
                  Not used/DK/NA

    (g)   Looking in national newspapers
                  Interview resulted
                  Used but no interview
                  Not used/DK/NA

    (h)   Looking in trade papers
                  Interview resulted
                  Used but no interview
                  Not used/DK/NA

(i)   Asking friends or relatives

Interview resulted
Used but no interview
Not used/DK/NA

(j)   Using private employment agencies

Interview resulted
Used but no interview
Not used/DK/NA

(k)   Getting in touch with trade union offices

Interview resulted
Used but no interview
Not used/DK/NA

(l)   Asking welfare organisation, social workers and probation officers

Interview resulted
Used but no interview
Not used/DK/NA

(If man made redundant in last job (see q. 46) ask q. 58(a).
Note: in all these questions 'last job' = last full time job before the
spell of unemployment that the man was in when he was selected for
the sample in week ending 1 October

58(a)   Did you receive a redundancy payment?

Yes
No
D.K.
NA/Refusal

(If 'yes' to q. 58(a) ask 58(b))

58(b)   How much did you receive? *(interviewers write in amount to nearest pound to 3 figures, using 998 for D.K. and 999 for NA/Refusal)*

59   In your last job what was your typical 'take home' pay each week? *(Write in amount to nearest pound to 2 figures, use 97 for 97+, 98 for D.K. and 99 for NA/Refusal)*

60   Did your pay in your last job often vary much?

        Did not often vary
        Varied between £0 and 4.99
        Varied between 5 and 9.99
        Varied between 10 and 14.99
        Varied between 15 and 19.99
        Varied between 20 and more
        D.K.
        NA/Refusal

61   Does the figure you gave for the take home pay in your last job include overtime earnings? *(If it does not but overtime was normal the figure should be adjusted to take this into account. Otherwise code as follows)*

        No overtime worked
        Overtime earnings   £0 to £4.99
                          £5 to £9.99
                          £10 to 14.99
                          £15 to £19.99
                          £20 or more
                          D.K.
                          NA/Refusal

62   Including overtime earnings what is the lowest level of weekly take home pay you would accept? *(Write in amount to nearest pound to 2 figures etc.)*

63   *(Ask if man now back at work)* How much do you earn in your present job? *(Write in amount to 2 figures as for q. 59)*

64   *(If man not back at work)* How much do you expect to earn when you get a job? *(Write in amount to 2 figures as for q. 59. If man says he does not expect to get a job, code 99 as for NA)*

65 Taking what you/expect to earn/earn at present how much of this are you prepared to spend on travel? *(Interviewers insert appropriate wording)*

£.....................p

(Interviewers convert this figure into a % of the income quoted in reply to question 63 or 64)

None
0–1.9%
2–3.9%
4–5.9%
6–7.9%
8–9.9%
10% or more
D.K.
NA/Refusal

66 For how long are you prepared to travel to work each day? (maximum, single journey)

up to ½ hour
more than ½ hour up to 1 hour
more than 1 hour up to 1½ hours
more than 1½ hours up to 2 hours
more than 2 hours up to 2½ hours
more than 2½ hours
D.K.
NA/Refusal

67(a) Are you prepared to do a job that would regulary involve being away from home?

Yes/Depends
No
D.K.
NA/Refusal

(If 'yes' to q. 67(a), ask 67(b))

67(b) Over a period of a year, for how long are you prepared to be away?

(i)   one to two weeks
(ii)   a month
(iii)   between a month and 3 months
(iv)   between 3 and 6 months
(v)   between 6 months and a year
(vi)   D.K.
(vii)   NA/Refusal

(If 'no' to 67(a), ask 67(c))

67(c)   Could you say why you say 'no'? *(Write reason for post coding)*

68(a)   Would you be prepared to move house in order to get work?

Yes/Depends
No
D.K.
NA/Refusal

(If 'no' to q. 68(a) ask 68(b))

68(b)   Could you say why you say 'no'?

(i)   Age
(ii) Housing problems
(iii) Children's schooling
(iv) Friend's and relatives
(v)   Other reasons (Specify

.....................................)

(vi) D.K.
(vii) NA/Refusal

69   How many times have you moved your home during your working life? *(Write in number to 2 figures, treating 20+ as 20, D.K. as 98 and Refusal as 99)*

JOB SATISFACTION

70   Could you say in order of preference which of the following you consider the most important qualities for a job to possess?

(a)   Interesting and satisfying work
(b)   Good pay
(c)   A good foreman/boss
(d)   Good working conditions (includes hours and answers like 'working indoors' or 'working outdoors'
(e)   Satisfactory workmates/colleagues
(f)   Adequate off-work facilities (e.g. canteen, sports club etc.)
(g)   Others (Specify...

....
(h)   Nothing (nothing else) important
(i)   D.K.
(j)   NA/Refusal

71   To what extent do you anticipate that you will be able to satisfy these requirements in the kind of job you usually do?

> Anticipate full satisfaction
> Anticipate some satisfaction
> Unlikely to satisfy
> Sure not to satisfy
> D.K.
> NA/Refusal

72(a)   Do you think the people at the Employment Exchange have considered all the facts in your case?

> Yes
> No
> D.K.
> NA/Refusal

(If 'no' to q. 72(a) ask 72(b))

72(b)   Could you explain why you say this? *(Write in answer for post-coding)*

73(a)   Do you think the exchange staff could have done more to help you find a job?

> Yes
> No
> D.K.
> NA/Refusal

(If 'yes' to q. 73(a) ask 73(b))

73(b)   What are the most significant ways in which you think the staff could have given you more help?
(Write in up to 2 ways for post-coding)

74(a)   *Coding key for Government training*

    A.   No information about Government training
    B.   Completed training course
    C.   Had information on Government training but did not apply
    D.   Applied for training, rejected at Employment Exchange
    E.   Applied for training, rejected by panel
    F.   Applied but withdrew application
    G.   Applied, awaiting results of application
    H.   Successfully applied but rejected while on course
    I.   Successfully applied but withdrew from course
    J.   Still attending
        NA/Refusal

74(b)   *Variable Q (see chart)*
        (a)   Suggestion of the Employment Exchange
        (b)   Others' suggestion/own initiative
        (c)   D.K.
        (d)   NA/Refusal

74(c)   *Variable R (see chart)*
        (a)   Government Training Centre
        (b)   Industrial Rehabilitation Unit
        (c)   Any other kind (Specify.......
                ....)
        (d)   More than one kind (Specify..
                ....)
        (e)   D.K.
        (f)   NA/Refusal

74(d)   Why did you not apply? *(See chart for applicability, writing in for post-coding, using D.K. or N.A. where applicable)*

74(e)   Why did you not complete the course? *(applicability etc. as for q. 74(d))*

75.   The Personal Disturbance Questionnaire cannot be reproduced for copyright reasons (for further information see Foulds op. cit.)

GENERAL BACKGROUND INFORMATION

76(a)   Is your father still alive and under 65? *If man says 'yes', ask him* do you see him once a month (or more).
                              Yes
                              No/he's dead/he's over 65
                              D.K.
                              Refusal

76(b)   *(If 'yes' to q. 76(a) ask 76(b))*
                        Is he........
                              in work?
                              unemployed?
                              neither/any other answer?
                              D.K.
                              NA/Refusal

77(a)   Have you any brothers you see once a month?
        (or more often)
                        Yes
                        No
                        D.K.
                        NA/Refusal

77(b)   *(If 'yes' to q. 77(a) ask 77(b))* Are any of those brothers who you see
        unemployed?
                        He is/they are all unemployed
                        One (Some) are unemployed but not all
                        He is/they all are employed
                        D.K.
                        NA/Refusal

78(a)   Are you, or have you ever been, a member of a trade union?
                        Yes
                        No
                        D.K.
                        NA/Refusal

        If 'yes' to 78(a) ask 78(b)
78(b)   Do you believe in trade union membership?
                        Yes
                        No
                        D.K.
                        NA/Refusal

Bibliography

Abel Smith, B. and Townsend, P. (1965) *The Poor and the Poorest* London, Bell.

Acton Society Trust (1962) *Redundancy*, London, Acton Society Trust.

Atkinson, A.B. (1970) *Poverty in Britain and the Reform of Social Security*, Cambridge, Cambridge University Press.

Bakke, E.W. (1933) *The Unemployed Man*, London, Nisbet.

Beveridge W. (1912) *Unemployment: A Problem of Industry*, London, Longman.

Booth, C. (1902) *Life and Labour of the People of London*, Vol. 5. London.

Bosanquet, N. and Standing, G. (1972) 'Government and Unemployment 1966–70: A Study of Policy and Evidence', *British Journal of Industrial Relations*, Vol. 10(2).

Bosanquet, N. and Doeringer, P. (1972) 'Is there a Dual Labour Market in Great Britain', Unpublished paper.

Brechling, F. (1967) 'Trends and Cycles in British Regional Unemployment', *Oxford Economic Papers*, Vol. 19.

Daniel, W.W. (1968) *Racial Discrimination in England*, Harmondsworth, Penguin Books.

Davies, J. Gower (1972) *The Evangelistic Bureaucrat*, London, Tavistock.

Davis, A. (1946) 'The Motivation of the Under-Privileged Worker' in Whyte, W.F. (ed.)' *Industry and Society*, New York, McGraw Hill.

Department of Employment (1971) *People and Jobs*, London, HMSO.

——, (1972) *Training for the Future*, London, HMSO.

Department of Employment Gazette (formerly Ministry of Labour Gazette) reports on a survey of unemployed men in 1966 issues pp. 156–7 and 385–7; statistics taken from various issues; report on the publication of People and Jobs, December 1971; report on the publication of Training for the Future, February 1972.

Department of Employment (1972) *Unemployment Statistics: Report of an Inter-Departmental Working Party*, Cmnd. 5157.

Department of Trade and Industry (1971) *Trade and Industry*, July issue.

Faith, N. (1971) 'The Endless Dole Queue', *Sunday Times*, 26th September,

Foulds, G.A. (1965) *Personality and Mental Illness*, London, Tavistock.

Franke, W.H. (1965) 'The Long-term Unemployed', Chapter 3, of J.M. Becker ed. *In Aid of the Unemployed*, Baltimore, Johns Hopkins Press.

Greater London Council (1969) *Greater London Development Plan*, London, GLC.

Hall, R.E. (1970) 'Why is the Unemployment Rate so high at Full Employment', *Brookings Papers on Economic Activity*, No. 3.

Hauser, M.M. and Burrows, P. (1969) *The Economics of Unemployment Insurance*, London, Allen and Unwin.

185

HMSO (1963) *The North-East: A Programme for Regional Development and Growth*, London, Cmnd. 2206.

—, (1967) *Shipbuilding Enquiry Committee 1965–66*, London, Cmnd. 2937.

Holland, S.S. (1965) 'Long-term Unemployment in the 1960s', *Monthly Labour Review*, Vol. 88(9).

Howe, G.M. (1970) *National Atlas of Disease Mortality*. London, Nelson.

Hunter, L.C. (1963) 'Unemployment in a Full-Employment Society', *Scottish Journal of Political Economy*, Vol. 10.

Jahoda, M. et al (1972) *Marienthal: The Sociography of an Unemployed Community*, London, Tavistock.

Kahn, H.R. (1964) *Repercussions of Redundancy*, London, Allen and Unwin.

Lawton, R. (ed.) (1970) *Merseyside*, London, Longmans.

MacKay, D.I. et al (1971) *Labour Markets under Different Employment Conditions*, London, Allen and Unwin.

Ministry of Social Security (1965) *Circumstances of Families*, London, HMSO.

Mukherjee, S. (1972) *Making Labour Markets Work*, London, PEP Broadsheet 532.

North-East Development Council (1970) *Skills in North-East England*, Newcastle, NEDC.

Olsson, B. (1963) 'Employment Policy in Sweden', *International Labour Review*, May Issue.

O.E.C.D. (1963) *Labour Market Policy in Sweden*, Paris, O.E.C.D.

Paish, F.W. (1968) 'How the Economy Works' *Lloyds Bank Review*, April Issue.

Pilgrim Trust (1937) *Men without Work*, London.

Rehnberg, B. (1969) 'Active Manpower Policy in Sweden', *Three Banks Review*, June Issue.

Reid, G.L. (1971) 'The Role of the Employment Service in Re-Deployment', *British Journal of Industrial Relations*, Vol. 9(2).

Reubens, B. (1970) *The Hard to Employ: European Programs*, New York, Columbia University Press.

Richardson, H.W. and West, E.G. (1964) 'Must we always take Work to the Workers', *Lloyds Bank Review*, January Issue.

Sinfield, A. (1968) *The Long-term Unemployed*, Paris, O.E.C.D.

—, (1970) 'Poor and Out of Work in Shields' in P. Townsend ed. *'The Concept of Poverty*, London, Heinemann.

Sobel, I. and Wilcock, R.C. (1966) *Placement Techniques for Older Workers*, Paris, O.E.C.D.

Sonquist, J.A. and Morgan, J.N. (1964) *The Detection of Interaction Effects*,

Monograph No. 35, Survey Research Center, University of Michigan.

Stein, R.L. (1963) 'Work-History, Attitudes and Income of the Unemployed', *Monthly Labour Review*, Vol. 86(12).

Stevenson, O. (1973) *Claimant or Client*, London, Allen and Unwin.

Supplementary Benefits Commission (1971) *Supplementary Benefits Handbook*, Revised Edition, London, HMSO.

Thirlwell, A.P. (1972) 'Government Manpower Policies in Great Britain', *British Journal of Industrial Relations*, Vol. 10(2).

Wedderburn, D. (1964) *White Collar Redundancy*, Cambridge, Cambridge University Press.

—, (1965) *Redundancy and the Railwaymen*, Cambridge, Cambridge University Press.

West Midlands Regional Study (1971) *A Developing Strategy for the West Midlands*, Birmingham, WMRS.

Woolf, M. (1967) *The Housing Survey in England and Wales*, London, HMSO.

Index

age
  and crime, 67
  as factor in employment prospects, 94, 95, 96
  and job mobility, 75–6, 77, 132
  and length of unemployment, 10–11, 41–3, 64, 69, 132, 139, 140, 141; in AID analysis, 125, (Coventry) 113, 116, (Hammersmith) 117, 121, 127, 135, (Newcastle) 121, 122, 123, 125, 127
  and marital status, 54
  and past experience of unemployment, 70–2
  and possibility of training, 100, 144
  and reason for termination of employment, 72–3
  and redundancy pay, 88, 114
  and sickness and disability, 41, 44, 48
  and wages, 78, 81
  and willingness to move, 97, 98, 114, 131
age distribution of samples, 35–6
aircraft industry, in Coventry, 21, 22, 24
areas selected for research, 15
Asians, in Coventry, 54, 128, 137, 154
automatic interaction detector programme (AID), 110–12

birthplace, for British-born, within or without survey area 14, 36, 52
  and job mobility, 77
  and length of unemployment, 137–8; in AID analysis, 126, (Coventry) 114, 115, 117,
(Hammersmith) 117, 118, 120, 121, (Newcastle) 122, 123, 124, 125
  for those born overseas, see immigrants

car ownership, Coventry, 18–19
children: number of, and length of unemployment, 13, 54–5
clerical workers, 23, 28
construction industries
  in London, 26
  unemployment in, 23, 65
  wages in, 78
Coventry, 15, 18–24, 38, 61
  AID results for, 113–17, 127–8
  for particular aspects of unemployment in Coventry, see under the individual subjects
crime
  convictions for, and length of unemployment, 66–7, 69, 138; in AID analysis, (Coventry) 115, 117, (Hammersmith) 121, (Newcastle), 122, 125
  record of, as factor in employment prospects, 94, 95, 96
  types of, 68
Criminal Records Office, 13, 35, 39, 65, 154, 155

Department of Employment, 8, 16
  statistics from, 6, 10, 14, 36
Department of Health and Social Security
  letter to members of sample from, 138, 155
  records from, 39, 43, 154
Development Areas, jobs exported from Coventry to, 24

189

disability
    change of occupation caused by,
        46
    change of registered occupation
        caused by, 62, 136
    as factor in employment pros-
        pects, 47, 95, 96
    main types of, 45
    percentage of those with, having
        treatment, 43, 46
    quota system for employment of
        those with, 128, 133–4, 150
    registration of, 44, 45–6
    self-assessed, and length of unem-
        ployment, 4, 43–8, 64, 133;
        in AID analysis, 125, 126,
        (Coventry) 115–16, 127,
        (Hammersmith) 120, 121,
        (Newcastle) 121, 122, 125,
        127
    and wages, 78
    see also sickness
Disabled Resettlement Officers, 133,
    150
domestic problems, as factor in em-
    ployment prospects, 95, 96

earnings-related supplements to un-
    employed benefit, 82, 83, 87,
    149
economic factors in unemployment,
    1–2, 126–7
    relation between social factors
        and, 6, 9, 140–2
education of sample, 36, 38, 142–3
    and length of unemployment,
        56–60, 69
employers, selection of employees
    by, 8–9, 141
employment
    factors involved in prospects of
        getting, 94–6
    nature of, among qualities in job
        satisfaction, 102, 103
    percentage changes in numbers
        in, by sectors: Coventry
        sub-region and Great Britain
        (1961–6), 22; London

(1961–6), 25–6; Newcastle
    (1965–70), 32
methods of hunting for, 104–6,
    132; effectiveness of, 106–7
reasons for termination of, 72–
    4, 86
willingness to move to obtain, see
    willingness to move
employment agencies, private, 105,
    106, 146
Employment Exchanges
    attitude of sample to, 107–8,
        109, 145
    classification of unemployed by,
        62, 96, 136–7
    in job-hunting, 105, 106
    proposals for reorganisation of,
        145–8
    records from, 35, 39, 61, 62, 154
employment record, redundancy
    pay as reflection of, 117, 131
engineering
    in Coventry, 19, 21, 22; unem-
        ployment in, 23
    in Newcastle, 33

family allowances, 87, 130
family commitments, and length of
    unemployment, 55–6
family income supplement, 130
folklore and mythology of unem-
    ployment, 9, 55
frictional unemployment, 2, 6, 127
full employment, 9, 151–2

Hammersmith, 15, 25–30, 38, 61
    AID results for, 117–21, 127
    for particular aspects of unem-
        ployment in Hammersmith,
        see under the individual sub-
        jects
health and length of unemployment,
    11, 43–51, 69
    see also disability, mental health,
        sickness
household size, in Hammersmith, 29
housing
    in Coventry, 19; in Hammersmith,

29–30; in Newcastle, 34–5
  of sample, 37, 88–92, 93, 139
  and willingness to move, 98, 99,
    115

illiteracy, 143
  and length of unemployment,
    58–60
immigrants (born overseas)
  in Coventry, 18, 36, 53
  employment prospects for, 96
  in Hammersmith, 29, 36, 38, 53
  job mobility among, 77
  length of unemployment among,
    13, 52–4, 69, 137; in AID
    analysis, (Coventry) 114, 115,
    117, 128, (Hammersmith) 117,
    118, 120, 121, 127, 128, 135
incentives to work, 4–5, 13
income out of work, 13, 139
  compared with wages in last job,
    78–9
  and length of unemployment,
    79–80, 93, 130
  for income in work, see wages
Industrial Development Certificates,
  in Coventry, 23–4
interviews with sample, 35, 153–5
involuntary unemployment, 2–3
Ireland, immigrants from, 18, 29,
  36, 52

job mobility, 75–7, 96–9
  high P.D. scores and, 134
job satisfaction, questions on, 102–
  4

labour market, hypothesis of a dual,
  132, 137
labour turnover, in Coventry, 133
labourers, see unskilled workers
length of unemployment, 6, 14–15,
  37, 39–41
  as dependent variable in AID
    analysis, 111
  main determinants of: age, 41–3;
    convictions for crime, 65–8;
    education, 56–60; health,

53–51; marital status and family commitments, 54–6; place
  of birth, 52–4; see also under
  these headings
Liverpool, unemployment in central
  zone of, 43, 64
local authority housing, 89, 90, 91,
  92, 93, 115, 139
  in Coventry, 19; in Newcastle, 35
  over-represented in sample, 37,
    89, 90
London, employment and population changes in, 25–7

machine-tool industry, in Coventry,
  22, 24
malingering, 3
manual workers, percentage of population as, Newcastle, 34
  See also skilled manual workers,
    unskilled workers
manufacturing industries
  in Coventry, 19, 20–1, 24; in
    Hammersmith, 27–8; in Lon-
    don, 25, 26; in Newcastle,
    32
  wages in, 78
marital status of sample, 36, 37
  and length of unemployment, 54,
    69, 134; in AID analysis, 126.
    (Coventry) 115, 116, 117,
    (Hammersmith) 118–19, 120,
    121, (Newcastle) 124
mental health, 45, 50, 150
  and length of unemployment, 11,
    50–1, 69
  see also personal disturbance scale
mining, in Coventry region, 21, 22
mobility, see job mobility, willingness to move
motivation
  explanations of unemployment
    in terms of, 4–5, 14, 129–32,
    138
  indirect indicators of, 126
motor-vehicle manufacturing, in Coventry, 21, 22

Newcastle upon Tyne, 15, 30–5,
38, 62
AID results for, 121–5, 126–7
for particular aspects of unemployment in Newcastle, see under the individual subjects
newspapers, in job-hunting, 105,
106
non-manual workers
in Hammersmith, 36, 38, 135
length of unemployment among,
in AID analysis, (Coventry)
113, 116, (Hammersmith)
121, 128
see also occupations, registered
North Shields, reasons for termination of employment in, 73

occupations
percentages of sample in different, 65
reserved for disabled, 150
unemployment rates for different, 11–13
versatility between, of sample,
64
occupations, registered, of sample,
61
discrepancy between last job and,
62, 96, 136
and length of unemployment,
62–5, 134–6, 140, 144; in
AID analysis, 125, 126,
(Coventry) 113, 115, 116,
117, 127, 128, (Hammersmith) 117–18, 118–19, 121,
125, (Newcastle) 121, 122,
125, 127
and past experience of unemployment, 70
and qualities expected of jobs,
102–4
see also professional, non-manual,
skilled manual *and* unskilled
workers
owner-occupation of houses, 19, 35,
89, 90, 91

pensions, 80, 87
personal disturbance (P.D.) scale, for
estimating mental health, and
length of unemployment,
50–1, 134; in AID analysis,
126, (Coventry) 114, 117,
(Hammersmith) 118, 119,
121, 127, (Newcastle) 124
Poor Law approach to unemployment, 1, 149
population
age structure of, Hammersmith,
29
decrease of: Hammersmith, 29;
London 25; Newcastle, 30,
32
increase of, Coventry, 18
poverty: extent of, in sample, 83–6,
93, 138–40
privately rented housing, 19, 30, 35,
89, 90, 91
professional workers, employers, and
managers
in Coventry, 18; in Hammersmith,
28; in Newcastle, 34
see also occupations, registered
psychological problems, as factor in
employment prospects, 95
public transport, in Newcastle, 34

questionnaire, 156–84
interviewers administering, 153–
4
quota system
for employment of disabled, 128,
133–4, 150
for employment of elderly men?
145

racial origin, *see* immigrants
redevelopment, of centre of Newcastle, 31
redundancy, as reason for termination of employment, 72, 73
redundancy pay, 87–8, 139, 144
association of, with age, 88, 114,
139

question on acceptable length of
time and percentage of earnings to be spent on, 96–7

'unemployables', 1, 7, 8–9, 140
unemployed men and vacancies,
numbers of
in Coventry: (1968–72), 20;
(1971), 23
in Great Britain (1956–72), 10
unemployment
changes in rates of, by industry
groups: Greater London and
Great Britain (1961–6), 26;
Newcastle, Northern Region,
and Great Britain (1963), 31
length of, *see* length of employment
past experience of, by sample,
70–5
regional inequalities in, 6–7
unemployment benefit, 37, 38,
82–7 *passim,* 139
earnings-related supplement to,
82, 83, 87, 149
Unemployment Review Officers,
148, 151
United States
motivation of underprivileged
workers in, 4
unemployment in, 42–3, 72
unskilled workers (labourers)
disabled as, 48
Employment Exchanges and, 136,
147
numbers of vacancies for, compared with number unem-
ployed, 12, 23, 141, 147
percentage of, in sample, 36
as percentage of unemployed: in
Central London, 27; in Coventry, 23; in different areas,
11
skilled workers registered as, 62,
96, 136
specialisation among, 135
see also occupations, registered

'voluntary' unemployment, 2, 3–4,
5, 73–4, 92–3, 129–30, 135

wages
average for sample and for sample
areas, 37, 139
in Coventry, 19; in Hammersmith
29; in London, 29; in Newcastle, 34
figures stated to be acceptable for,
and length of unemployment,
80–2, 131
in last jobs of sample, 77–8; compared with out-of-work
income, 78–80
among qualities in job satisfaction, 102, 103
Wales: immigrants from in Coventry, 18
West Indians, in Hammersmith, 54,
137
willingness to move, or work away
from home, 96–9, 109
associated with age, 97, 98, 114
and length of unemployment, in
AID analysis, 126, 131–2,
(Coventry) 113, 114, 115,
117, (Hammersmith) 118, 119,
120, 121
wives, earnings of, 85, 87, 130
women
changes in number of, employed,
London and Great Britain
(1961–6), 26
employment rate of: in Hammersmith, 28; in Newcastle,
33
lower wages of, for unskilled
work, 141
working conditions, among qualities
in job satisfaction, 102, 103

youth unemployment, 16